IN THE
NATIONAL INTEREST

General Sir John Monash once exhorted a graduating class to 'equip yourself for life, not solely for your own benefit but for the benefit of the whole community'. At the university established in his name, we repeat this statement to our own graduating classes, to acknowledge how important it is that common or public good flows from education.

Universities spread and build on the knowledge they acquire through scholarship in many ways, well beyond the transmission of this learning through education. It is a necessary part of a university's role to debate its findings, not only with other researchers and scholars, but also with the broader community in which it resides.

Publishing for the benefit of society is an important part of a university's commitment to free intellectual inquiry. A university provides civil space for such inquiry by its scholars, as well as for investigations by public intellectuals and expert practitioners.

This series, In the National Interest, embodies Monash University's mission to extend knowledge and encourage informed debate about matters of great significance to Australia's future.

Professor Susan Elliott AM
Interim President and Vice-Chancellor,
Monash University

ISABELLE REINECKE

COURTING POWER: LAW, DEMOCRACY & THE PUBLIC INTEREST IN AUSTRALIA

MONASH
UNIVERSITY
PUBLISHING

Courting Power: Law, Democracy & the Public Interest in Australia
© Copyright 2023 Isabelle Reinecke

Monash University Publishing
Matheson Library Annexe
40 Exhibition Walk
Monash University
Clayton, Victoria 3800, Australia
https://publishing.monash.edu

Monash University Publishing brings to the world publications which advance the best traditions of humane and enlightened thought.

ISBN: 9781922979230 (paperback)
ISBN: 9781922979254 (ebook)

Series: In the National Interest
Editor: Greg Bain
Project manager & copyeditor: Paul Smitz
Designer: Peter Long
Typesetter: Cannon Typesetting
Proofreader: Gillian Armitage
Printed in Australia by Ligare Book Printers

A catalogue record for this book is available from the National Library of Australia.

The paper this book is printed on is in accordance with the standards of the Forest Stewardship Council®. The FSC® promotes environmentally responsible, socially beneficial and economically viable management of the world's forests.

COURTING POWER: LAW, DEMOCRACY & THE PUBLIC INTEREST IN AUSTRALIA

It's a steamy, overcast morning and the air is thick with heat. I'm at the northernmost inhabited point of Australia, on the low-lying Boigu Island in the Torres Strait, only a short boat ride to Papua New Guinea. It's a beautiful, sandy, mud and coral island threaded by freshwater river systems, surrounded by blue ocean, and filled with thick mangroves, dugongs, turtles and saltwater crocs. The crocs are coming inland more often these days, hungry and looking for dogs.

A fleet of small charter planes has just arrived at the island carrying more than twenty lawyers, court staff, and Justice Michael Wigney of the Federal Court of Australia. Kids have run down from the local primary school next to the single-runway airstrip to welcome the visitors, waving and clapping with excitement. The outsiders are here to be participants of history in the making. Guda Maluyligal traditional owners Uncle Pabai Pabai and Uncle Paul Kabai, and their communities on Boigu and Saibai islands, have launched a world-first climate change class action. They are suing the Australian Government for climate negligence in the Torres Strait—the first First Nations people in the world to sue their government in this way.

An hour after the planes arrive, Uncle Pabai is called as the first witness in the case. We're in the Boigu Community Hall, which has been painstakingly transformed by Uncle Pabai's extended family and community into a tropical facsimile of the Federal Court. Palm fronds have been macheted off trees, and some have their long green leaves wrapped carefully around the hall's big metal beams, while others have been woven into hanging vases decorated with bright red jungle geranium and white frangipani, and bunches of green bananas. A row of potted palms is set against huge sheets of satin that hang from the ceiling behind the judge in white, green and blue—the official colours of the Torres Strait, referred to locally as Zenadth Kes.

The seating for Uncle Pabai was carefully prepared the day before by his sister Aunty Diane Messa and wife Aunty Waimed Pabai, the plastic chairs wrapped in white satin, and double-stacked to avoid any embarrassment if one was to break. He sits at the front of the court, with Judge Wigney to his right.

The judge has eschewed the typical billowing black robes of regular court, preferring a casual, short-sleeved navy shirt, khakis and sandals. Uncle Pabai faces two rows of long tables of lawyers—his legal team, led by Fiona McLeod SC, is to his left, and the Australian Government's lawyers are to his right. Behind them sit Boigu community members and Elders who have come to watch this historic moment. The court has come to their land, to hear from their community. The government must sit and listen.

Uncle Pabai is a warm, softly spoken man, dressed unlike the judge in a dark suit set off with a vibrant green shirt and yellow tie. These are his clan colours, and reminiscent of his totem, the crocodile. Uncle Paul, his co-lead plaintiff and brother-in-law from Saibai, watches carefully from the audience. He is relieved he doesn't have to go first.

'The ancestors are very important for us,' Uncle Pabai explains to the court. 'Their knowledge, [their] understanding, passed on from generation to generation. They are giving us who we are today, to identify ourself. They are the most important people for us. If my community goes underwater, I will lose my identity from my land and I will lose every experience [the ancestors have] given to us because they will be no longer with us. This is why I'm saying my people will never [be] remove[d] from our land.' He pauses. 'Because of our ancestors.'

The reality of climate change is confronting here on Boigu. Massive, ancient beach almond trees and staggeringly large coconut palms have been uprooted as the shoreline has moved inland, their drying roots pulled from deep in the ground, left to die in the hot tropical sun. Huge seagrass fields, dinner for local sea creatures, are disappearing beneath the water. The once abundant and fat dugongs and turtles, totems and key sources of food for local people, are also dwindling, and getting skinnier. Once fertile agricultural land has turned to swamp. Parts of the island have absorbed so much salt during huge king-tide flooding that taro, sweet potato, cassava and watermelon, which have been sources of culture, sustenance and trade for generations, can no longer be grown there. When witness Uncle Boggo Billy from Warraber is asked later in the trial how he knows the water is getting warmer, he simply says, 'I put my hand in.' The increasing warmth of the sea here is undeniable.

The Guda Maluyligal nation includes Boigu, Saibai and Dauan. On a previous trip I'd taken to Zenadth Kes, Saibailgaw man Herbert Warsuan—a ranger and key witness in the case—had stood with me on the northern shore of Saibai during one of the island's long, exquisite sunsets. 'Do you want to know what Guda Maluyligal means?' he asked. He pointed at the strait between the island and Papua New

Guinea and made a 'C' with his fingers. 'That's *guda*,' he said. 'It means mouth or opening. This is where the spirits travel through so they can protect the mainland.' I couldn't help but shiver, thinking of how the people here were taking action that could end up protecting all Australians from the horrors of the climate crisis.

According to Torres Strait tradition, people are born with a totem animal, a constellation and a wind. The winds are changing too. On my way to Boigu, I found myself standing on the jetty on Narupai (Horn Island) with a young local ranger. We were facing east towards lush, green Waibene (Thursday Island) towering above the sea, and watching a storm rolling in. 'Wind's coming from the north,' the ranger explained. 'It's not meant to come at this time of year.' Now, the winds are blowing from the north too often, and at the wrong time.

Aunty Jen Enosa, a witness on Saibai, will later take the court to the northern beaches there, to show the judge where she and her aunties collected shells and crabs at low tide when she was a little girl. She will explain how beautiful it was before the seawall had to be built, how the winds used to arrive from Papua New Guinea on Christmas Eve, filling the air with the fragrant smell of flowers, marking when the dancing would begin. But the winds are changing there too. They don't come at Christmas anymore.

On Boigu, heavy drops of rain are pummelling the corrugated-iron roof of the community hall-come-court. At one point, Justice Wigney interjects, 'I'm sorry, Ms McLeod, I can't hear a word you're saying. It may very well be the rain on the roof that is creating these difficulties … Somewhat ironic.' It's meant to be the dry season.

Aunty Vera Auda and Uncle Lenny Gibuma, two senior Boigugal Elders, have already marked the beginning of formal proceedings. They welcome the outsiders to country, acknowledge their ancestors and Elders past and present, and present Justice Wigney with a yam branch with large, vivid green leaves—a symbol of peace. Children have brought their chairs from school and are sitting in the front row. They've had the fear of god put into them by their teachers, and they do not make a sound. Instead, quiet, bristling excitement fills the air.

'At its most basic, it is an abrogation of the social contract,' Fiona McLeod tells the court. She is one of Australia's top barristers, a leader of the national legal profession, past president of the Law Council and the Independent Bar Association, and chair of the Accountability Round Table. At no small expense, she and a small team, including Lindy Barrett from the Victorian Bar, are acting pro bono as Uncle Pabai and Uncle Paul's barristers, effectively donating upwards of a million dollars to their case. They have good reason to do so.

McLeod outlines the uncles' argument: 'The evidence that will be led in this case will show that the Commonwealth has and continues to ignore the dire and existential threat to the lives of its own citizens. Its failure to act is a failure of the fundamental duty of a government to protect its citizens and First Peoples from harm. It is a failure to protect fundamental human rights including the right to life and the right to self determination ... Torres Strait Islanders' culture is place-based. The traditional ways of life, knowledge and culture are inextricably connected to the islands. You cannot separate Torres Strait Islander culture from the islands themselves. The two are the same ...'

McLeod goes on to say that harm 'from climate change impacts on the Torres Strait has already been extremely significant. Islands are flooding more regularly and with greater volume; cemeteries have been flooded and ancestors' bones have been washed away; coastal erosion is widespread; reefs are dying; corals are bleaching and dying; fish, dugong, turtles and crays are affected; and the traditional hunting and gathering practices are being rendered obsolete ... The projected impacts of climate change in these islands will be catastrophic. There is the real potential of being forced to leave these islands, severing the unbroken cultural connection of thousands of years.'

Three weeks later, after time spent on Boigu, Badu and Saibai, and in Cairns, the court officials, lawyers and camera crews all head home, while the islanders remain to face the daily impacts of climate change on their way of life. It's been a whirlwind experience for everyone involved, demonstrating that everything is at stake for these communities. The words of Aunty McRose Elu, a senior Elder from Saibai and 2021 Queensland Senior Australian of the Year, ring in my ears: 'We come with anger, love and care.' Yes, people are angry, but also, and perhaps more importantly, they love and care for their country and their communities. This is what they're fighting for.

ON COUNTRY

In an earlier case-management hearing—where the court makes logistical and administrative orders in preparation for the main trial—Chief Justice of the Federal Court Debra Mortimer decided that the hearings should be split, so that community evidence could be heard 'on country'. This is a deeply significant decision. It means the court must go to the people, not the other way around. It recognises the court's role, as described by former chief justice of the High Court Gerard Brennan, 'to serve and protect not the governors but the governed'.[1]

Reflecting on the importance of on-country hearings in 2017, then justice Mortimer explained that the court has a lot to be proud of in the way it conducts its hearings on country. She said

> at the end of the day litigation is an exercise in persuasion. Proof is about persuasion, and context. You get all of those things from listening to evidence on country. And then of course aside from the actual context and the setting and the better understanding, the really well recognised difference in the way that Aboriginal and Torres Strait Islander peoples behave when they're talking about their country when they're on their country in comparison to how constrained they feel when they're in a courtroom situation—even if it's an informal courtroom in a hall. It's not the same for them and that is so obvious that it would have been a tragedy if we hadn't continued to build on what Justice [Martin] Moynihan did and continued the development of on country hearings.
>
> I don't think there's a single judge on our court that has done on country evidence who doesn't understand the value of it—it's absolutely critical. It's also a great privilege. You feel that you're sharing something that's very, very special. And I think that's part of what creates such a deep impression with the

judges because I think they understand that what they're hearing is a great privilege.

Both Anglo-European Australian culture and Aboriginal and Torres Strait Islander culture place great emphasis on ritual and ceremony in their own ways. People appreciate the importance of ritual and ceremony.[2]

When Friedrich Nietzsche said that time is a flat circle, he clearly wasn't thinking about Australian legal procedural history. Nonetheless, the origin of on-country hearings stretches back more than thirty years to the same place where this story began: the Torres Strait Islands.

In May 1989, justice Martin Moynihan of the Supreme Court of Queensland made the unprecedented decision, at the request of the plaintiffs, to hear evidence in *Mabo v The State of Queensland* on country rather than in the courtroom in Brisbane. Dubbing the trip 'The Great Northern Expedition',[3] the court heard evidence from sixteen elderly and frail witnesses on Mer Island, and another five witnesses on Thursday Island. It travelled and viewed the land and seas that Eddie Mabo and his co-plaintiffs laid claim to. According to one of the key barristers on the Mabo team, Bryan Keon-Cohen, the trip was 'a valuable exercise evidentially for the plaintiffs, and a significant and enjoyable event for the Court,

court staff, the lawyers, the Meriam residents, and various journalists who also turned up'.[4]

Justice Moynihan remarked upon the significance of opening the court in the council hall on Mer (also known as Murray Island) in 1989:

> Sitting here helps me to understand the evidence concerning Murray Island, its people, and its culture. And perhaps most importantly it, to a degree, enables the people of Murray Island to participate in the process of justice that is being worked out in these proceedings. You do that by your presence here this morning and in your participation in the work of the Court.[5]

The Queensland Government lawyers laboured under formal robes in the heat while on country, and at Mer they stayed 50 metres offshore in a 'hot, cramped, ugly looking barge'. Keon-Cohen later reflected that the 'sight of the Queensland team, robed, clambering into a dinghy each morning, and being rowed ashore was too reminiscent of certain past events to be pure chance! The gods are sometimes great!'[6]

Since the court's first 'Great Expedition', the practice of hearing evidence on country has become common in native title cases. It has also extended to other legal areas, including negligence class actions, as in *Pabai v Commonwealth*. This is a relatively unknown but telling legacy of the series of cases that culminated in the High Court *Mabo (2)* decision in 1992.[7] That case famously recognised that a group of Torres Strait Islanders, led by Eddie Mabo, held ownership of Mer, and that native title existed for all First Nations people in Australia. The signal it sent at the time was significant.

THE HIGH COURT AND AUSTRALIAN IDENTITY

The High Court's *Mabo* decision was just one in a series of highly consequential cases decided from the early 1980s to the late 1990s that recognised the changing reality of modern Australia. These judgments acknowledged hugely significant principles in the evolution of Australian national identity, in relation to First Peoples, the environment and political rights. They also unleashed a torrent of fury from opponents that in recent years has increased in intensity, and—more alarmingly—in impact.

Earlier, the constitutional principle that a healthy legal system is fundamental to democracy was securely bipartisan. Without an apolitical court system that cherishes its role as an independent arbiter of the rule of law, who has the power to hold even the most powerful in our society accountable to it? No-one. Attacking this principle is a recipe for democratic decay. A strong court system, one that ensures access, accuracy and transparency, enables democratic accountability between election cycles and should be revered and supported.

The bipartisan respect for our legal system began to kink when prominent, sustained, ad-hominem attacks on the judiciary reared up post-*Mabo*, fuelled by dissatisfaction with the outcomes of cases in the decade prior. With the systemic unravelling of judicial independence in the United States by conservative forces over the past fifty years, and the Benjamin Netanyahu government's controversial judicial overall in Israel this year, it is timely that we pause to remember the importance of legal principle in decision-making that impacts on democratic rights. In Australia we should celebrate the role of the High Court and judicial system in our democracy, not condemn it.

In 1980, before the transformative run of cases began, the High Court moved out of its two-storey, 1920s-era red-brick building in Melbourne's Little Bourke Street, and went to Canberra. Its new home was dramatic, lofty, itself an expression of an emerging national identity no longer bound so closely to Britain. They say beauty is in the eye of the beholder, or perhaps brutalism is an acquired taste. Respondents to a Heritage Focus Group undertaken by the court in 2011 variously described the edifice in Parkes

Place as an 'ugly concrete bunker' and 'theatrical and inspiring'.[8] I have come to love this severe building, the backdrop for seismic moments in Australian history like the *Mabo* and *Wik* decisions. It was popularised in contemporary culture by the award-winning 1997 movie *The Castle*. As the bumbling lawyer for Darryl Kerrigan, Dennis Denuto, famously implored the court, 'In summing up, it's the Constitution, it's Mabo, it's justice, it's law, it's the vibe.'

The High Court is constructed of huge panes of glass and cream concrete, and has an interior atrium flooded with natural light. It is surrounded by native plants and set against the waters of Lake Burley Griffin. It is a marked departure from the stripped-back classical Melbourne building. The 'heroic architecture' is said to embody 'the spirit of a national building and faith in the future'.[9] The High Court sits in the line of sight of the Australian Parliament, within architect Walter Burley Griffin's National Triangle, but stands alone, linked only to the National Gallery. Its location is meant to represent the separation of powers.

Three years after shifting north, the High Court made one of its most high-profile decisions, now known as *Tasmanian Dams*. The case marked the final chapter in an epic and politically fraught battle between conservationists and the Tasmanian Government. This is now seen as the beginning of Australia's green political movement, which included the establishment of the world's first 'green' political party,[10] and the start of a new era when international agreements signed by governments could be relied on to shape domestic policy.

In *Tasmanian Dams*, the High Court decided that the Bob Hawke government had the power to stop the Tasmanian Government from constructing the Franklin Dam at its proposed World Heritage–listed site. Michael Black, one of the barristers involved in the case, later said of the atmosphere of the court, 'It was almost palpable, the sense of history and importance.'[11] The court found that the 'external affairs power' in the Australian Constitution validated Commonwealth legislation that gave effect to the World Heritage Convention and protected the sites listed in it. Today, large parts of Australia's national environmental law depend on this decision for its constitutional validity.

Despite his dissenting opinion, chief justice Harry Gibbs wrote that he was not concerned about whether the court could rightfully make such a significant decision in the politically heated context. He carefully clarified that the decision was about the law, not policy. Political heat did not make the substantive legal issues a no-go zone:

> No lawyer will need to be told that in these proceedings the Court is not called upon to decide

whether the Gordon below Franklin Scheme ought to proceed. It is not for the Court to weigh the economic needs of Tasmania against the possible damage that will be caused to the archaeological sites and the wilderness area if the construction of the dam proceeds. The wisdom and expediency of the two competing courses are matters of policy for the governments to consider, and not for the Court. We are concerned with a strictly legal question—whether the Commonwealth regulations and the Commonwealth statute are within constitutional power.[12]

A few years later, the symbolism of the High Court's still-new, grown-up home became more literal. The court, along with the country, unshackled itself from the United Kingdom and the Privy Council, along with its legal precedent and ability to overrule the highest Australian court, with the *Australia Act 1986*. The High Court could finally 'take heed of specifically Australian conditions in developing the law', and shape it 'in line with contemporary community values and the international community at large'.[13]

In 1992, the same year as the *Mabo* verdict, the High Court delivered another hugely significant judgment in *Australian Capital Television v Commonwealth*. Eight commercial news broadcasters had sued the Commonwealth, arguing that laws limiting advertising during elections were invalid. The Paul Keating government of the time asserted that the laws were designed to reduce the influence of money in politics, due to the great expense of broadcasting political advertisements. But the court agreed with the broadcasters that restricting political advertising in this way unduly restricted the ability of Australians to communicate on politics and therefore make decisions about who to elect. The court recognised that the Constitution must contain an implied freedom of political communication, or the foundational constitutional tenants of representative government would not be operable.

The limits of this so-called implied freedom were further teased out two years later in *Lange v Australian Broadcasting Corporation*. In that case, then New Zealand prime minister David Lange sued Australia's national broadcaster for defamation. The ABC was unsuccessful in its attempt to rely on the implied freedom as a defence. The court clarified that the Constitution did not imply an individual's 'right' to free political communication but rather acted as a limit on the power of executive government to 'burden' free political communication.

As current High Court Justice Stephen Gageler explained in 2022, the court's role in the context of the implied freedom is supervisory. This gives the legislature leeway in how to meet its policy objectives, but ensures that constitutional imperatives are not sacrificed.[14]

The genesis of the *Mabo* action could be said to date back to 1965, when Eddie Mabo was working as a groundskeeper at James Cook University in Townsville and historian Henry Reynolds arrived to take up a lectureship. The two men hit it off, and Reynolds began researching the history of Indigenous Australian–settler relations. Reynolds later recounted an exchange he had with his friend, explaining that Mabo

> would often talk about his village and about his own land, which he assured us would always be there when he returned because everyone knew it belonged to his family. His face shone when he talked of his village and his land.
>
> So intense and so obvious was his attachment to his land that I began to worry about whether he had any idea at all about his legal circumstances … I said something like: 'You know how you've been telling us about your land and how everyone knows it's Mabo land? Don't you realise that nobody actually owns land on Murray Island? It's all Crown land.'
>
> He was stunned … How could the whitefellas question something so obvious as his ownership of his land?[15]

During the same period, Barbara Hocking, the 'intellectual architect of the *Mabo* case', had begun to work on an argument for common law recognition of 'traditional Aboriginal title'. This went against the advice of her Monash University supervisor, 'an esteemed senior academic who simply could not accept her central premise'.[16] Hocking presented her paper 'Is Might Right? An Argument for the Recognition of Traditional Aboriginal Title to Land in the Australian Court' in 1981 at a James Cook University conference. At the conclusion of the forum, Hocking was briefed by Eddie Mabo and Father David Passi. Their case was filed in May the following year in Brisbane.

Famously, a little over ten years later, the High Court found that the common law concept of terra nullius, which had been used to justify the British Crown's 'ownership' of Australia, had no factual or legal basis. The court agreed with Eddie Mabo and his co-plaintiffs that they held property rights ('title') in the Murray Islands that had not been extinguished, and to which, 'as against the whole world', they were entitled to 'possession, occupation, use and enjoyment'.[17]

The federal government has exclusive power under the Constitution to enact laws under thirty-nine broad concepts listed in section 51, from marriage to quarantine. States have power over whatever is left. That list reflects the national priorities of Australia at Federation in 1901. It does not, for example, include some of today's enormously important national priorities, including the environment. Gough Whitlam in 1957 recommended that the government 'make more use' of the external affairs power in the Constitution to 'extend its legislative competence'.[18] That was an appalling proposition to federalists, the conservative side of politics since Federation,[19] who believed that strictly limited Commonwealth power ensured 'federal balance' in the system. This concept does not appear in express terms in the Constitution.[20] The idea is that by 'balancing' the federal and state governments, citizens are protected 'from the power of a unitary state', which 'enhances their freedoms while maintaining order and stability'. For small-l liberals, this diffusion of power is seen as an 'unnecessary obstruction' to social reform.[21] Changing the nation's approach to an issue occurs much more slowly if it must be done state jurisdiction by state jurisdiction, rather than in one fell swoop at the federal level.

The High Court's decision in *Tasmanian Dams* followed principles established by the court in 1920,[22] and which had been 'lamented by federalists ever since'.[23] It found that the Commonwealth had the authority to enact environmental legislation via the external affairs power. This prompted great consternation over the potential implications for federalism: was the 'federal nature of the polity, the very survival of a federal Commonwealth', imperilled?[24] Well, no, as it turned out. The court clarified the limits of the external affairs power a few years later in *Burgess*.[25] Community opinion was not with the federalists, and the objections failed to gain mainstream traction. But the fear had conservatives redrawing battle lines to include the court, and laying the seeds for the Samuel Griffith Society.

The implied freedom cases aroused concerns about the court 'overstepping' its role. But it was *Mabo* that really spurred the anti-court brigade into action. It may be little known or understood outside of a small political-legal circle, but the case sparked an extraordinary reaction. Chief justice Gerard Brennan described it at the time as 'ill-informed' criticism of the Australian judiciary. It was an attempt to put it back in its box.[26]

THE ANTI-COURT CAMPAIGN

The *Mabo* decision was groundbreaking—and controversial among some—for its reference to texts of academic historians and Aboriginal custom. The High Court had joined the real world. But it was the words of justices William Deane and Mary Gaudron that were latched onto. In their joint judgment, the justices described dispossession in 1804 on the

Hawkesbury River as illustrating 'the first stages of the conflagration of oppression and conflict which was, over the following century, to spread across the continent to dispossess, degrade and devastate the Aboriginal peoples and leave a national legacy of unutterable shame'.

Perhaps anticipating the reaction to come, they explained:

> In those parts of this judgment which deal with the dispossession of Australian Aborigines, we have used language and expressed conclusions which some may think to be unusually emotive for a judgment in this Court.
>
> We have not done that in order to trespass into the area of assessment or attribution of moral guilt. As we have endeavoured to make clear, the reason which has led us to describe, and express conclusions about, the dispossession of Australian Aborigines in unrestrained language is … the full facts of that dispossession …[27]

The day after the judgment was delivered, the Australian Mining Industry Council told the *Australian Financial Review* that 'anything which increased the restrictions imposed in the mining industry in access to land for exploration was an undesirable development'.[28]

Grown from the seeds of discontent in *Tasmanian Dams*, *ACTV* and *Lange*, but in direct response to the *Mabo* decision, the Samuel Griffith Society was established later in 1992 by former chief justice Sir Harry Gibbs, former National Party senator John Stone, businessman Hugh Morgan and legal academic Greg Craven. With it came 'a purely ideological approach' to the Constitution and a successful dissemination of 'their once radical views'. They are 'now de rigueur on the right, and have spread into the wider culture'.[29]

A year after the *Mabo* decision, the Samuel Griffith Society held its first conference, during which two 'scathing' and 'aggressive' papers attacking the High Court were delivered by high-ranking members of the legal profession. The Association of Mining and Exploration Companies Inc., with permission from the society, began publishing copies of the papers as pamphlets.[30]

'Judicial independence does not exist to serve the judiciary; nor to serve the interests of the other two branches of government,' then chief justice Brennan remarked when reflecting on the role of the courts at the Australian Judicial Conference in Canberra in 1996. 'It exists to serve and protect not the governors but the governed.'[31] While the courts have never been immune to criticism, nor should they be, by this time a different sort of public campaign was underway.

In her seminal book on the subject, *The Campaign against the Courts: A History of the Judicial Activism*

Debate, Dr Tanya Josev details the extraordinary campaign by politicians and pastoralists to attack the High Court when it made decisions contrary to their interests and ideology. These attacks were not a sophisticated debate about proper judicial interpretation methods, although those arguments took place in legal circles too. Instead, the campaign adopted the American moniker of 'judicial activism'. It levied it as a derogatory term against any High Court decisions it disagreed with. As Josev writes, 'the charge of activism has provided the paradigm through which [High Court] decisions have been interpreted at the *expense* of substantive public discussion'.[32]

Incumbent prime minister John Howard and the New Right's 'anti-elites' political strategy of the mid-1990s was designed to pit 'elite-aligned special interests' against an 'average' Australia. This strategy, coupled with the emergence of Pauline Hanson's narrative that 'Indigenous activists' were elites, 'created the conditions for the High Court to be implicated' when it was inevitably called on to adjudicate further land rights disputes.[33] Nine months after the Howard government's election in early 1996, the *Wik* case was delivered. If *Mabo* was the match set to the kindling of discontent, *Wik* was the conflagration.

In *Wik*, the court was asked to decide whether the leases granted by the Crown to squatters during the 1800s, in an attempt to exert control over their grazing activities, extinguished native title rights. The extent of these leases across the country reflected the massive dispossession of Indigenous people by pastoralists. By the early 1990s, they covered a vast swathe of the country: over half of Queensland and the Northern Territory, and almost half of Western Australia, South Australia and New South Wales.[34] The court found that native title rights could 'co-exist' with pastoral leases, that the leases had not 'quashed' native title held by the Wik and Thaayorre peoples in their land, as had been hoped by those benefiting from pastoral leases.[35] Opponents of Indigenous land rights who were confident of *Mabo* being overturned were bitterly disappointed; 'pastoralists, miners, National Party members, and State Premiers were incensed'.[36] Their response was ferocious.

The attacks came from parliamentarians first. Deputy prime minister Tim Fischer, Queensland premier Rob Borbidge and Victorian premier Jeff Kennett 'eviscerate[d] the Court for its decision'. Judges were attacked ad hominem and for their perceived political leanings. Borbidge described the judges who had found in favour of the Wik people a 'historic pack of dills' and 'an embarrassment'. Fischer and Borbidge made barely veiled attacks on justice Michael Kirby's sexuality. Both men decried the majority judgment as judicial activism, with Borbidge arguing that this activism had begun with *Tasmanian Dams* and the implied freedom cases that followed.[37]

Prime minister Howard effectively endorsed these views by commenting that he understood Queensland's serious concerns about judicial activism. Echoing his anti-elites electoral campaign narrative, he then began to pit 'sectional interests supposedly preferred by the High Court' against the 'national interest'.[38] Feminism, Indigenous rights, latte-sipping and chardonnay-drinking urbanites, and 'establishment media' were the problem. The High Court was painted as hostile to the mainstream and part of the cabal.

Ironically, the High Court's role and integrity as an institution of democracy was attacked by the very people who claimed to be protectors of the rule of law. From there, a campaign of popular media and commentariat attacks was born. Judges were labelled as bogus, pusillanimous, evasive, plunging Australia into an abyss, pathetic, gripped by mania for progressivism, intellectually dishonest, undermining democracy, feral, basket weavers.[39] Laughable, until you realise the impact on the High Court's perceived integrity as a bastion of democracy.

Attacks on the High Court died down under chief justice Murray Gleeson, who served for roughly the period that the Howard government was in office. The court wasn't condemned when it upheld the validity of its predecessors' approach to land rights and the implied freedom of political communication. Instead, the lull 'on a pure results-oriented analysis' coincided with the court making decisions that largely upheld the agenda and legislation of the Howard government.[40]

Lower courts weren't spared, however. New Right–associated journalists and commentators turned their attention to law-and-order matters in criminal courts and refugee appeals to the Federal Court. Leading the charge was columnist Janet Albrechtsen and the News Limited papers. Albrechtsen wrote on the subject almost weekly from 2002 to 2008. She described judges as engaged in a 'war on democracy' and undermining the separation of powers by attempting to 'impose their elitist causes upon the electorate'.[41]

LAWFARE

Attacks on the High Court have since continued, sharpened and expanded in focus. The columnist Paul Sheehan took aim at anyone who initiated litigation regarding refugees. In an article in *The Sydney Morning Herald* in 2011, and which is still quoted with praise by conservative magazine *The Spectator Australia* today,[42] he wrote:

> Ideological lawfare is now clogging the entire legal system in the name of refugee rights. The people

enmeshed in this campaign against Parliament range from the Chief Justice of the High Court, Robert French, to the ideologues toiling in the lower courts and refugee tribunals.[43]

The 'lawfare' language was taken from the United States, where the epithet had been levelled against Guantanamo Bay detainees and their legal representatives, who sought to challenge the lawfulness of indefinite military detention and torture.[44]

Sheehan was responding to the High Court's decision in *M70 v Commonwealth* earlier that year. This stymied the Kevin Rudd/Julia Gillard government's Malaysia Solution—a plan to deport 800 Afghani people to Malaysia, despite Australia's international human rights obligations. Malaysia was not a signatory to the relevant international convention. Conditions for refugees there were described as 'nothing short of appalling with harassment and violence part of the refugee community's daily experience, and the threat of arrest a constant'. The court agreed with the seemingly straightforward argument that the government did not have the appropriate power under the relevant legislation to deport asylum seekers to Malaysia. But instead of just attacking the court, Sheehan targeted those he described as 'the people and legal activists' who 'successfully circumvent democracy by waging lawfare'.[45]

The setback was deeply embarrassing for the Gillard government. While the decision was 'largely greeted with praise within the profession', the prime minister's response was 'immediate and personal'. She singled out chief justice Robert French for alleged inconsistency. She accused the court, 'tellingly if bizarrely',[46] of making a decision that represented a 'missed opportunity to send a message to asylum seekers not to risk their lives'.[47] Then attorney-general Robert McClelland quickly issued a statement later that evening. Unlike the approach of attorney-general Daryl Williams post-*Wik*, McClelland reiterated the government's respect for the court and toned down the prime minister's response: 'The Government respects the High Court, its judges and the role it performs as the ultimate umpire on legal matters.'[48]

The Opposition publicly demanded the prime minister 'leave the High Court alone',[49] but turned its attention to the lawyers representing people seeking asylum. When again in government, Peter Dutton, then immigration minister, described them as 'un-Australian'. He told Alan Jones on 2GB radio, 'These lawyers have been playing the game with these people who are willing participants, and we're a generous nation, but we're not going to be taken for a ride.'[50]

Next up for criticism were communities seeking to access the courts to protect the environment from harm.[51] Following major debate regarding the climate impacts of controversial conglomerate Adani's Carmichael coal mine in Queensland (Adani is now Bravus Mining & Resources), the MacKay Conservation Group and its lawyers at the Environmental Defenders Office filed a case against federal environment minister Greg Hunt in January 2015. On 4 August, the Tony Abbott government settled the case, acknowledging that Hunt had not lawfully exercised his power to decide whether to approve the mine.[52] But Abbott, attorney-general George Brandis and the Association of Mining and Exploration Companies went on to describe the action as 'lawfare', 'sabotage' and 'gaming legislation'.[53] Prime minister Abbott commented:

I'm not for a second saying that people should not be able to exercise their legal right, I'm not for a second criticising the courts, what I am being very critical of is the tactics of some element of the green movement and their apparent ability to play games and to game the system.[54]

The Federal Court responded through a spokesperson: 'The orders were not made after a hearing. There was no judgement. There were no findings. The orders were made by consent; that is, with the agreement of the parties to the litigation.'[55]

The outcome was embarrassing for the government and problematic for its agenda. The legal reasons for it were benign enough for the government to have conceded and settled the case. It simply recognised the minister's basic duty to uphold the rule of law. But by seeking to access the judicial review mechanism fundamental to Australian democracy, environmentalists were accused of 'gaming the system'. Brandis took aim at environmental legislation for laying a 'red carpet for vigilante litigation'.[56] He omitted mention of the Federal Court's power to dismiss vexatious litigation.[57] The Queensland Resources Council called on the government to 'step up and close the loopholes' that allowed judicial review.[58]

Two years earlier, in December 2013, the federal government had announced $43.1 million in funding cuts for community legal services.[59] In the face of a huge backlash, by March 2015—two months after the MacKay Conservation Group filed its case against Adani—the attorney-general reversed the cuts, except those applicable to the Environmental Defenders Office.[60] Not much later, the government amended the *Environmental Protection and Biodiversity Conservation Act 1999* 'without notice and in a manner plainly designed to shield their proposals from effective public scrutiny'.[61] This included an unsuccessful attempt to limit the law of standing in environmental cases—that is, who has the right to bring a case on an issue.

Unlike other jurisdictions around the world, groups representing marginalised or victimised people in Australia are rarely able to bring litigation on their behalf, to shield them from the emotional and financial stress of being the 'David' in court battles with 'Goliath'. Koalas and river systems, however, cannot defend themselves in court, meaning that Australian environmental law has allowed others to bring cases in their place since 1999. In a speech to the Australian Administrative Law Forum National Conference in 2016, attorney-general Brandis described this as enabling the 'possibility of abuse … that is, "lawfare" … a kind of social, political or environmental warfare' via 'the law and the institutions and processes of the law'. He went on to argue that judicial enforcement of the law via 'relaxed' standing provisions is 'not actually about the rule of law so much as the rule of lawyers and the interests of lawyers'. Brandis asked the forum:

> Do we perhaps need a body of public interest lawyers whose sole focus is to act as rule of law sentinels— policing governmental action and litigating the otherwise un-litigated? In effect, relaxed or non-existent standing rules move us closer to that scenario—that nightmare dystopia in which the only legitimacy that any government action can have will be had in a litigated outcome.[62]

Similarly, the Australian adverse costs system is not in sync with the approaches taken by our global kin in public interest matters. It operates to serve the interests of those who would prefer to avoid accountability in court. Addressing this prohibitive procedural feature by enabling a more robust democratic system was the underlying principle that motivated me to establish Grata Fund. The impact of the costs system, and how out of step it is with similar jurisdictions internationally, is little understood beyond public interest lawyers in Australia. Adverse costs are the fees payable by the party that has lost a case, to cover the legal costs of the winner. Usually, this will be about 75 per cent of the bill, although sometimes, where a litigant has abused the litigation process, the court will order the loser to pay close to 100 per cent of their opponent's legal fees. For example, in June 2023, disgraced former soldier Ben Roberts-Smith was ordered by agreement to pay the legal costs of the media outlets he unsuccessfully sued for defamation, estimated at about $25 million.

This system is perfectly fair in most ordinary litigation, where there are limited implications for broader public interest—say, those pursuing personal rights. Or, similarly, commercial disputes where, it's worth noting, the losing entity can claim a tax deduction for the expense. However, carte-blanche adverse cost orders are a prohibitive risk for litigants seeking to hold governments or corporate actors accountable in the public interest. Under the current system, even people who have strong cases and excellent pro-bono legal teams need to be prepared to lose their homes and entire bank balances to bring public interest litigation. Usually—and quite understandably—these people baulk at bringing a case. Democracy is left worse off as a result, with litigation that seeks to hold even the most powerful accountable to the rule of law never seeing the light of day.

Unlike other approaches around the world, from the United Kingdom to Hungary, Germany and the Netherlands, to the United States, Brazil and South Africa, public interest litigants in Australia do not have reliable protection. Despite numerous federal and state inquiries calling for reform since 1995, there has been little progress. Some tinkering at the edges by way of maximum cost orders in the Federal Court and the NSW Land and Environment Court remain unpredictable in application, unaffordable in quantum and have failed to address the core problem. The federal government is currently considering whether to reform this system for victims/survivors of sexual discrimination, as recommended by the Respect@Work inquiry. However, several of the models being considered by the Attorney-General's Department, such as costs neutrality and applicant's choice models, are insufficiently nuanced and are likely to cause as many problems as they attempt to solve.

At a fundamental level, our current system fails to recognise the importance of public interest litigants to the maintenance of our democracy. Opponents to reform claim they want to avoid opening the 'floodgates' of litigation. These opponents forget, perhaps, that the court would maintain its power to order a litigant to pay costs where they have abused legal processes. More importantly, though, this argument fails to recognise that, if there is a flood of meritorious cases not being heard by the courts, maybe that is something that should be rectified in a thriving democratic system.

PUBLIC INTEREST ON TRIAL

It was not until 2020, when the rights of First Nations peoples were again at stake, that the attacks on the court returned to the deafening crescendo of the *Mabo* and *Wik* era. The case determined the inalienable citizenship rights of First Nations people. The *Wall Street Journal* summarised it as 'essentially a clash between Australia's recognition of historical wrongs against its original inhabitants and its growing modern hostility toward outsiders perceived to be a threat to society'.[63] The case arose in the context of forcible deportations by the Department of

Home Affairs of non-citizens for failing a 'character test' under the *Migration Act*. These deportations had increased ten-fold in the decade prior. More than 2500 people were returned to New Zealand despite many having moved to Australia as children and considering themselves Australian.[64] The policy led to 'long-simmering resentment' with Australia's neighbour,[65] with prime minister Jacinda Ardern remarking, 'I have a specific objection to the fact that we have people being deported from Australia who we consider to be Australians.'[66]

Daniel Love and Brendan Thoms were caught up in this scheme. Both men are Aboriginal Australians who have lived most of their lives in Australia, although Love was born in Papua New Guinea and Thoms in New Zealand. They each fell foul of the *Migration Act* character test in their thirties, after being convicted of crimes that attracted prison terms of more than twelve months. Having completed those sentences in 2018, both men were detained by Home Affairs personnel, had their visas revoked, and were told they would be deported to their birth countries. Their cases were heard together and are now known as *Love and Thoms*. In February 2020, the High Court decided that the government did not have the power to deport either man because 'Aboriginal Australians (understood according to the tripartite test in *Mabo [No 2]*) are not within the reach of the "aliens" power'.[67]

The decision was monumental. It built on the common law in *Mabo* by recognising the special status of First Nations people in a new constitutional context. Eddie Synot, Wamba Wamba man and public law academic at Griffith University, explained to the media:

> *Love* matters in the same way *Mabo* matters—they're both important to who we are as a nation of peoples. Despite its limitations, *Mabo* finally offered recognition—formally at least, according to the common law—of First Nations where it had previously been denied. The power and importance of that recognition—and its continuance in *Love*—cannot be underestimated.[68]

The response among those who disagreed with the decision was swift. *The Australian* published a series of columns taking aim at the court.[69] The face of each judge and whether they had decided 'for' or 'against' the 'shameful ruling' illustrated legal affairs editor Chris Merritt's column. He wrote:

> Four judges went off on a frolic: Geoffrey Nettle, Michelle Gordon, James Edelman and Virginia Bell. [Susan] Kiefel was steadfast, backed by Stephen Gageler and Patrick Keane … The judges in the majority are massively out of step with community

values and the core principle of equality before the law.[70]

Two days later, Merritt reported in *The Australian* that Institute of Public Affairs (IPA) polling showed 45 per cent of respondents agreed any reference to race should be removed from the Constitution— a harbinger of the 2023 Voice referendum's 'No' campaign. 'The court's decision, which was opposed by Chief Justice Susan Kiefel,' he wrote, 'has triggered concern about whether the Constitution can safely be amended to recognise indigenous Australians.'[71] On the same day, conservative law professor James Allan wrote for the paper that 'our top judges are vying for the title of the most activist judges in the common law world'.[72]

Janet Albrechtsen, who became chair of the IPA in 2019, was less reserved:

With scant regard to the law, the majority of the High Court dreamt up a legally bogus exception based on race to exclude two men from the normal application of our non-citizens laws. Four judges imagined that their personal preference to tinker with the Constitution matters more than our constitutional right to change our founding document by a referendum, and only by a referendum ... Four judges created new law, undermined the rule of law, altered the words of the Constitution, snubbed the power of parliament and appointed themselves philosopher kings in our democracy.[73]

A few days later, in a piece titled 'High Court's Racist Ruling Is a Low Blow to Equality and Democracy', *Australian* columnist Dr Jennifer Oriel wrote:

> The first priority of government is to keep citizens safe. The High Court appears to have abandoned the principle in an apparent pursuit of social justice. The court's new 'belongers' can commit violent crimes against Australians without fear of deportation if they have the right blood. If the goal of the High Court four was to sow the seeds of backlash against indigenous Australians, they have done a sterling job of it.[74]

Meanwhile, Caroline di Russo, who three years later would be elected WA Liberal Party president, wrote in *The Spectator Australia*:

> Interestingly, each of the majority judgments has the hallmark of being reverse-engineered or, at the very least, appear to be tarted-up versions of the applicants' submissions. The reasonings are long, soupy and Twister-esque in their evolution. And they

play out like good ol' progressive activism running roughshod over the constitution to sculpt a palatable and suitably woke outcome.[75]

The outcry was so intense, and so inappropriate, that the Australian Bar Association (ABA) released a statement that read in part:

> Debate and commentary should … at all times respect the position of the courts and the rule of law. Inflammatory language which attacks the integrity of judges who have taken an oath to serve the public tends to undermine the public's confidence in the courts. Confidence in the courts and the rule of law is vital to the continuation of our peaceful community.
>
> The ABA considers that some of the commentary about last week's decision of the High Court in *Love and Thoms v The Commonwealth* went beyond the bounds of robust criticism.[76]

Eminent Aboriginal academic Professor Marcia Langton also responded to the reaction in a column in *The Australian*:

> Following the *Mabo (No 2)* decision in 1992, the response from the Coalition, business, mining, farming and grazing leaders, along with the usual pack of shock jocks, was hysterical and, above all, wrong.

So, too, the response during this past week from the hard right and the far right to the High Court decisions in *Love v Commonwealth* and *Thoms v Commonwealth*: hysterical, wrong and misleading.[77]

Nevertheless, the ground had been laid for the campaign against the courts to go up a notch.

THE POLITICS OF APPOINTMENTS

Conservatives recognised the importance of two High Court seats becoming available in 2020, on a bench of seven, with appointees holding their positions until the age of seventy-two. The IPA described the post-*Love* appointments as the 'most consequential since Federation'.[78] Along with the IPA, Professor James Allan began to call for the appointment to the bench of 'explicitly capital-C conservatives'.[79] Criticising the fact that three of the four judges in majority for *Love and Thoms* were appointed by the Coalition government, Allan wrote that

the supposedly 'don't fiddle with our written Constitution', anti-judicial activism, pick con-stitutional conservatives political party in this country, the Liberal party, has proved to be one of the most useless, ineffective, asleep at the wheel conservative parties in the democratic world … The

Attorney-General needs to call the Solicitor-General in and tell him, order him, to take the position in every single future case that Love was wrongly decided. The judges will hate it. The lawyers will hate it. It should be done all the same; indeed this should be the attitude as regards the ever burgeoning implied rights case law too … Meantime, with three upcoming vacancies to the High Court maybe this Morrison government might take its core responsibility here a bit more seriously.[80]

The government, meanwhile, attempted to thread a needle, conflating 'black letter' lawyering with the antithesis of 'judicial activism'. Government MPs were described as 'sounding the alarm ahead of two High Court vacancies amid concerns judges hand-picked by former attorney-general George Brandis have ventured into judicial activism, straying from a "black letter" approach to constitutional interpretation'.[81]

Among a series of speeches decrying the *Love and Thoms* decision at a Samuel Griffith Society conference later in 2020, then senator Amanda Stoker condemned the High Court's 'judicial activism' and described the majority decision as 'truly disturbing'. She called for the case to be challenged after the upcoming retirement of two members of the High Court.[82] Stoker also outlined a plan for how conservatives in Australia could replicate The Federalist

Society, the conservative and libertarian legal advocacy organisation in the United States to which the current hyper-partisanism of the US Supreme Court is widely attributed.

Professor George Williams, then dean of UNSW Law School, and Supreme Court Justice Judith Kelly, then president of the Judicial Conference of Australia, separately responded to the calls for 'capital-C conservative' appointments as inappropriate. Professor Williams said it was likely to undermine the public's confidence in the judiciary and lead to a US-style appointments process.[83]

Brandis responded to the outcry in a column for *The Spectator Australia*:

> When I recommended to Cabinet the appointment of Susan Kiefel as Chief Justice, and the other three judges who were appointed on my recommendation (Nettle, Gordon and Edelman), I was concerned about one thing only: their eminence and ability as lawyers. Some right-wing polemicists ... have recently demanded that judges be appointed not because they are the best lawyers, but because of their politics ... Applying an ideological test for judicial appointments—thereby politicising the one arm of government whose authority depends upon public confidence in its political impartiality—would be a deeply unconservative thing to do.[84]

Noting these responses in his Samuel Griffith Society speech, Senator James Paterson attempted to reframe the cries for politicisation by claiming that critics were merely 'calling for the appointment of originalist judges who will use the original meaning of the Constitution as a guide through which they approach cases'. He then expressed his surprise that several 'eminent members of the legal establishment mistakenly assumed that constitutional conservatives were advocating for judges to be appointed according to their political (rather than judicial) views', adding: 'Perhaps it is the use of the term "capital-C conservative" which has confused them. Labels should not matter.'[85]

In an editorial later that year, *The Australian* warned then attorney-general Christian Porter, who was tasked with appointing judges to the High Court, that he

must wear responsibility for his choices, which will help define his political fortunes. The aliens case [*Love and Thoms*] did little to enhance the standing of former attorney-general George Brandis, who appointed two of the majority judges to the decision. Free of political distractions, Mr Porter should seek a legal conservative with strong adherence to the original intention of the Constitution and the black letter of statute.[86]

Labels do matter, though. Originalism is the 'arch-conservative' constitutional judicial method,[87] prominent in the United States, that relies on the original meaning of the text in its historical context to interpret the law. As the High Court itself said in 2013:

Debates cast in terms like 'originalism' or 'original intent' (evidently intended to stand in opposition to 'contemporary meaning') with their echoes of very different debates in other jurisdictions are not to the point and serve only to obscure much more than they illuminate.[88]

Its closest relative in Australia is 'legalism',[89] which in its simplest form considers the legal text as primary. Regardless, confining the substantial and nuanced judicial theory of 'legalism' to a vague aspiration for 'black letter' lawyering is superficial at best. Despite the furious responses to *Love and Thoms*, there is little—if any—serious jurisprudential analysis that suggests the decision was anything *but* legalist or even 'black letter' in approach.

Interestingly, chief justice Gleeson, whose court suffered relatively fewer public attacks on judicial activism grounds, did something differently to his immediate predecessors, chief justices Anthony Mason and Brennan. Gleeson built a narrative that his court's approach was 'legalistic'. Josev argues this helped to insulate his court by wrapping it in the 'unimpeachable veil' of chief justice Owen Dixon's legacy. This is regarded as 'beyond reproach, such that any jurists accused of straying far from Dixon's course may be regarded as a heretic' in Australia. Josev argues that the Mason and Brennan courts unquestionably saw themselves as part of its inter-pretative method and 'keepers of Dixon's flame'. However, Mason viewed legalism as 'an inadequate explanation of judicial methodology that cloaked the judicial reasoning process'.[90]

What Mason and Brennan perhaps failed to do was appreciate the degree to which attempts to 'uncloak' the judicial reasoning process needed to be pitched as a natural part of Dixon's legacy. Revealing a misjudgement of the legacy of the response that was to come, Mason said at the time that criticism would be 'a small price [to] pay' for creating 'a stronger sense of constitutional awareness' among the com-munity and 'a more accurate appreciation of the issues arising for decision'.[91] By failing to cultivate the legalist moniker or explain their most significant decisions in those terms, he and Brennan departed from the court's general tradition.[92] In so doing, they may have opened themselves and their courts— however unfairly—to attack from superficial but powerful criticism.

Legalism today is 'synonymous for a judge carrying out his or her duties'. Josev and others argue, however, that Dixon's definition of 'strict and complete legalism' has been desiccated and stripped of its nuance.[93] Instead, it has become a 'powerful legitimising device to be employed to shield the Court from criticism'.[94]

Amanda Stoker's calls for *Love and Thoms* to be relitigated after the appointment of new justices to the High Court were answered quickly. As a result of the *Love and Thoms* case, a number of people held in detention for deportation by Home Affairs became eligible for release. In an attempt to reopen the decision in *Love and Thoms*, the government appealed the release and visa reinstatement of Shayne Montgomery, a Waka Waka and Mununjali man. This put the High Court in a difficult position. Professor Gabrielle Appleby explained:

Because of the nature of some of the criticism of the *Love* case ... [there] will certainly be a perception that, should [the judges in *Montgomery*] overrule the *Love* decision so soon after it was decided, this is at least partly explicable by reference to the political ideology of the judges and the new appointments to the bench. This perception would be detrimental to public confidence in the independence of the High Court.[95]

The matter was ultimately heard by the High Court in April 2022. The next month, the Australian political landscape changed with the election of Anthony Albanese's Labor government. By August, the government had withdrawn its appeal against the reinstatement of Montgomery's visa. This released the High Court from its potentially uncomfortable position. Conservative legal commentators responded by arguing the decision not to pursue *Montgomery* risked politicising the court.[96] Stoker, by then a political commentator for *Sky News*, wrote that the decision was 'a disturbing signal the Albanese government is not serious about ensuring the integrity of Australia's migration program, and is happy to outsource significant parts of it to Aboriginal communities and their many and varied decision-making methods'.[97]

IMPLIED FREEDOM UNDER THREAT?

It is fair to say that the Australian legal community has long looked at aspects of the US judicial system as distasteful and, at times, disturbing, even before the latest Trump-era controversies: publicly elected lower court judges, the spectator sport of Supreme Court appointment processes, clear political campaigns and counter-campaigns for 'left' or 'right' judicial appointees, and open confrontation between the judicial and executive branches of government.

As justice Kirby told the American Bar Association at a conference in 1998:

> The prize for the worst examples in a developed country in this *genre* of political attack on the judiciary must go to the United States of America. Of particular concern ... has been the appearance of federal political leaders, looking around for themes for their electoral campaigns, selecting the easy targets of the judiciary as a means of promoting themselves as tough on law and order ... One of the features of the United States attacks on the judiciary which is most disturbing to an outsider is the way they have been followed up by removal from office, or threats of impeachment, of judges who require popular retention or re-election votes. Another concern is the complete misrepresentation of judicial opinions and serious over-simplification of complex issues ... The truth and the detail about controversial cases tend to elude headstrong politicians on the campaign trail.

So the call by deputy prime minister Tim Fischer, published on the front page of *The Age* in March 1997 in the wake of *Wik*, for 'capital-C conservative' appointments to the court, might have been seen as a misguided aberration by a politician who didn't know any better. Fischer's successors, Abbott and Brandis, were more tactical in their attacks. But Fischer's early calls, echoed in the demands of the IPA and Allan decades later, have taken root.

Coincidentally, two High Court appointments needed to be made later the same year as *Love and Thoms*. Justice Simon Steward and Justice Jacqueline Gleeson were appointed by attorney-general Porter. Despite the apparently bipartisan distaste for the 'hyper-politicisation' of the American judicial system, the *Australian Financial Review* reported that 'the Morrison Government has put a conservative stamp on the High Court with the appointment of two justices who are expected to shift the dynamic of the court to the right'. Justice Steward, in particular, was 'the favoured candidate of Victorian conservatives who promoted his credentials as a black-letter lawyer'. The IPA claimed a win, its executive director John Roskam commenting: 'These are very good appointments which will curb the High Court's adventurism.'[98]

Justice Steward is perhaps already living up to the hopes of his champions. Within a year of sitting on the bench, he raised scepticism about almost three decades of precedent on the implied freedom of political communication in a single opinion. In *LibertyWorks*, he wrote that

it is arguable that the implied freedom does not exist. It may not be sufficiently supported by the text, structure and context of the Constitution and, because of the continued division within this Court about the application of the doctrine of structured proportionality, it is still not yet settled law. The division within the Court over so important an issue may justify a reconsideration of the implication itself.[99]

This was a surprising observation, given that there had been no submissions before the court on this point. Other justices described the freedom as 'well settled' in the same case.[100] Acknowledging his duty not to decide on matters that are not before the court, Justice Steward appeared to invite future applicants:

In such circumstances, it is my current duty to continue to apply it faithfully. Any consideration of the existence of the implied freedom should, if necessary, be a matter for full argument on another occasion.[101]

The Centre for Comparative Constitutional Studies held a seminar the following year, marking thirty years since the implied freedom was first recognised. Professor Dan Meagher, Chair of Constitutional Law at Deakin Law School, remarked on Justice Steward's decision, commenting that

the proposition that the implied freedom is still not settled law is rather dubious; at least, since the High

Court's unanimous decision in *Lange* in 1997. Both the legitimacy of the implication and the test used in its application have been settled doctrine of the Court … it seems to me a unanimous judgement of the court and an unbroken line of authority since then. Too late now to … question its legitimacy.[102]

However, Meagher recognised that part of the test applied by the court when assessing whether a law falls foul of the implied freedom was the subject of 'quite reasonable disagreement' between two analytical camps on the bench.

University of Melbourne Laureate Professor Adrienne Stone agreed that the implied freedom is settled law. She doubted 'that it is much endangered in the short to medium term' but remarked that

we should not think that the freedom of political communication is wholly secure. On the contrary, in my view, the persistence of interpretive disagreement gives rise to a temptation that may last a long time to revisit the foundational question of the doctrine's legitimacy.

Indeed, 15 years ago when I first developed this account of interpretive disagreement, I speculated— and it really did seem a speculation then—that *Roe v Wade*, a case also attended by deep interpretive disagreement, might one day be overruled despite its subsequent affirmation in a long line of cases.[103]

Perhaps ironically for those calling for a more 'black letter' approach on the High Court, Professor Stone argued that the 'excessive legalism of *Lange*'— resulting in the two analytical camps referenced by Meagher—is what has led to any perceived ability to undo the doctrine in the future.[104] She argues this overly legalistic approach was 'unmistakably driven by a perceived need to shore up the legitimacy of the doctrine' in *ACTV*.[105] This has, she suggests, 'discouraged attention to the values on which its decisions inevitably rest, and in so doing has deprived itself of the tools it needs to develop freedom of political communication in a coherent manner'.[106] The impact of this approach can arguably be seen in recent decisions where the court's engagement with the substantive democratic values underlying the disputes is extremely limited.

For example, after the Australian Federal Police (AFP) raided her home and seized private phone data in June 2019, journalist Annika Smethurst brought an action that went to the heart of representative government. Smethurst had authored articles online and in print for *The Daily Telegraph* revealing a highly secret plan to give the Australian Signals Directorate covert powers to spy on its own citizens. In *Smethurst v Commissioner of Police*, she argued the

AFP's warrant was invalid for three reasons, including that the warrant 'impermissibly burdened' the implied freedom of political communication. The court did not need to address that argument, as it agreed with Smethurst that the warrant was invalid on the basis of an argument made earlier in her case. The Australian Human Rights Commission, however, made submissions as an intervener in the case. It argued that the court should consider the importance of freedom of political communication in the matter, given the fragility of press freedom in Australia that had been revealed by the raid. Despite this, the case was decided without substantive engagement with the implied freedom and the constitutional principles that underpin it.

A month earlier, the Federal Court (immediately below the High Court in hierarchy) *had* considered the freedom when it contemplated the validity of another AFP raid in *ABC v Kane (No 2)*. That raid took place a day after Smethurst's home came under assault. It extended over eight hours at the ABC's Sydney headquarters, following whistleblower reports it aired about war crimes perpetrated by Australian armed forces in Afghanistan. Sounding alarm bells for those supportive of press freedom, the court found the AFP raid was valid because the purpose for which it was sought was generally justified. The court found the raid did not burden the freedom of political communication sufficiently to be ruled invalid. In considering the ABC's case, the court relied on the High Court's reasoning in Bob Brown's successful challenge to Tasmanian anti-protest laws. There, Justice Gordon summarised, the implied freedom only exists to the minimum extent necessary to maintain representative government.[107]

Similarly, in 2014 the High Court declined to consider a challenge to the controversial *Al Kateb* decision made a decade earlier that indefinite offshore detention of 'stateless' people is legal.[108] The court dismissed the case after setting an extremely high factual bar to hear it. Sam* (*I've used a pseudonym to protect his identity), the man who brought the case with the assistance of pro-bono law firm Human Rights for All, does not know where he was born, suspecting he was taken to Western Sahara as a newborn. As an infant, he was trafficked by child sexual abuse networks throughout numerous countries. Eventually, he fell in with criminal gangs in Europe. Wanting to escape this life, and to get as far away as he could imagine, he made his way through refugee camps to Australia by boat. Despite the immigration minister agreeing he was a genuine refugee, he was never to be settled into the community as per government policy regarding refugees who arrived in Australia by boat. By the time of his case, he had languished in detention for nine years. Deeply traumatised, he was unable to provide a consistent time line of his life. Despite extensive investigations, the minister failed to establish the man's country of origin or to find another country willing to accept him due to his unknown birthplace. Sam's lawyers argued there was no real prospect of his country of birth being established or another jurisdiction willing to take him in. The court disagreed, dismissing the case on the grounds that the possibility of his removal to another country had not been exhausted. Sam went on to live in detention for another decade. In mid-2023, he was finally released on a bridging visa by the Albanese government.

Avoiding the substantive issues in dispute may be helpful for courts in seeking to appear impartial in a media environment where their decision-making will otherwise be compared to judicial activism. Unfortunately, in reality, the long-term effect of doing so tends to disproportionately benefit conservative interests. It weakens the judiciary's ability to exercise its democratic duty to hold governments accountable to the law. This limits the potential impact of judgments to clarify the law. It also affects the way in which barristers and lawyers advise their clients, how lower courts make decisions, and who is promoted to the upper echelons of the judiciary. More broadly, in relation to Australia's constitutional democracy, this is disturbing the important balance between the legislature, executive and judiciary, and weakening the power of our democracy's in-built accountability tool: the courts.

During an interview at the Cambridge Faculty of Law in 2011, the late, eminent Australian constitutional scholar Leslie Zines summed up the issue when describing the approach of chief justice Dixon, considered to be the father of strict legalism in Australia in the 1950s:

> [He] said that it's the only way for a court to behave— the only way you could trust a court is if it was concentrated in looking only at legal considerations, but, of course, he did not do that. I believe he pretended to do that.

Zines went on to explain that, because a constitution is loosely worded and 'intended to endure for ages to come', it contains broad and general language that should not be read as if it were an 'ordinary Act'. He argued that judges need to be aware of the choices they have.

> Once you are in the High Court you can come to several different conclusions, all of which are rational and, therefore, you should ask, 'Why am I going this way rather than that way?' and the law itself will not be the deciding factor. You will have to look at questions of social desirability or justice.[109]

There is always a balance to be found between the government and the courts that oversee its decisions. The risk of excessive black letter law is rarely discussed, but real. Edwin Cameron, former justice of the Constitutional Court of South Africa, argued in the High Court of Australia 2017 Public Lecture that the effective functioning of the judiciary and the survival of the rule of law within a democracy demand a political environment that openly reinforces 'moral engagement and moral choice in expounding constitutional values and protecting constitutional mechanisms'.[110] Reflecting on the failures of the South African judiciary in enabling apartheid to continue, Cameron warned that, in the absence of the operation of foundational attributes and methods of democracy, the efficacy of courts as conduits of legal power is deficient or undermined.

The viability of courts in democracies, Cameron went on to argue, is strengthened when the mainstay procedural elements of democracy realised via fair and free elections, freedom of speech and accountability, are maintained in a 'vibrant and functioning form'. He should know, having seen first-hand how an overly legalistic approach to the judicial role can lead to gross democratic abuses. He explained:

South African judges under apartheid sought by recourse to strict legalism to deny their exercise of choice and to elude moral responsibility for the choices they made. They failed. In each case the option is to acknowledge that moral engagement with the choices that interpretation of words and exposition of values entails is unavoidable or to deny that the choice exists at all.[111]

Acknowledging the essential foundational role of legalism, Cameron said that, referring to the judiciary,

we all *start off* as exponents of legalism ... [it is] the necessary precondition of our trade, our common starting point. It has to be: for we recognise that words have meaning, that this lays bounds to the quest for understanding, and that language, even when contested, is not indeterminate.

But, he clarified, legalism

is only the start of the judge's task. It cannot be the end. For lawyering unavoidably entails an embrace of value that formal analytical and conceptual technique cannot strip away, and constitutionalism only more ... [in] the end, we cannot escape the moral call of law and the institutional responsibility it entails; we cannot seek to abide by technical rules and prescripts that eschew value; and we cannot deny the wider possibilities and the deeper promises—as well as the deeper duties—that the law casts upon us all.[112]

IDEOLOGICAL ROT

The impact of the campaign against the judiciary since the 1990s has not been limited to the High Court. The Administrative Appeals Tribunal (AAT) has been the first line of judicial review for government decision-making since 1976. It was established to 'bring the rule of law to the level of primary decision-makers'.[113] The AAT is a critical part of Australia's transparency infrastructure, tasked with adjudicating freedom-of-information disputes which underpin the media, dynamic political opposition, and independent voices. In recent years, however, it has become 'notoriously politicised' by appointments.[114] Some of the most damning impacts of this politicisation were felt among people seeking asylum, who had wildly differing chances of having a visa rejection overturned depending on which tribunal member heard their case.

It was reported in 2022 that people seeking appeals for protection visas were 'almost twice as likely to be knocked back if they [came] before a tribunal member appointed by the former Coalition government', even when controlling for other variables.[115] One tribunal member, Jennifer Strathearn, who had been appointed by attorney-general Brandis, resigned in early 2022, objecting to the extent of appointment politicisation under attorneys-general Christian

Porter and Michaelia Cash. In a submission to a 2020–21 Senate inquiry into the AAT, she explained:

> Unfortunately, some of these AAT appointees have lacked sufficient qualifications, have obvious conflicts of interest, have not performed to the required standards, have caused backlogs in AAT reviews due to incompetence or lack of motivation, and some have been paid high remuneration for achieving precious little or anything of use to the AAT or its work. This has amounted to blatant cronyism and is now widely understood in Australian political and administrative circles to be the case. One cannot help but draw a conclusion that it may be incumbent upon this cohort of persons to do the current government's bidding, rather than perform an objective, accountable role in the AAT according to the rule of law.[116]

Later in 2022, with the AAT's reputation 'irreversibly damaged',[117] Attorney-General Mark Dreyfus announced it would be abolished and replaced with a new body. An expert advisory group, headed by former High Court justice Patrick Keane, is overseeing the process, with legislation expected to be introduced in late 2023 or the following year.

Two recent examples suggest that the anti-judiciary campaign has hit its mark. When the IPA celebrated the appointment of Justice Jacqueline Gleeson in

2021, it introduced a degree of partisan cheerleading more akin to contested US judicial appointments than the generally politically disinterested Australian system. In 2011, Liberal MP Julian Leeser had called for the Samuel Griffith Society to 'move from being a learned debating society to becoming a much more direct influence in the public debate of our nation'.[118] So perhaps it should have been little surprise that Griffith Society secretary and Coalition donor Stuart Wood joined the official celebration for the 'deeply conservative (both in his personal views and judicial approach)' Simon Steward at the Melbourne Italian restaurant Becco in 2020.[119] Then, Attorney-General Dreyfus's unprecedented decision to entirely disband the AAT, rather than attempt to patch it up, suggests that ideological rot had perverted the fifty-year-old institution beyond repair.

A DEMOCRATIC INSTITUTION

The long-term impact on democracy of concerted, sustained efforts by media commentators, lobby groups and parliamentarians to undermine the judiciary is hard to precisely pinpoint. The appointment of a High Court justice celebrated by ideologically motivated lobbyists, and the need to entirely disband a tribunal that has operated for over fifty years, are both worth pause for thought. Unless the courts' political independence and authority are championed by the legal and political mainstream, the consequences could be more serious than was anticipated when the early campaign against the courts began.

What to do about it? On the one hand, overstating the risks only serves to feed the campaign and provoke outraged commentary, potentially enlivening a counter-campaign that could chase us all down an internecine rabbit hole towards the situation in the United States. But ignoring it with dignified silence, as the court itself has largely done, and is rightly bound by tradition to do, may just give the critics comfort in the urgent world of hyper-partisan contemporary politics. It is this partisan immediacy that makes the attacks against the court so toxic. Perhaps, then, it is on us as a society to remember and celebrate the role of the High Court and judicial system in our democracy, and create a cultural bulwark around it.

Courts aren't just there to settle divorces, sentence law-breakers and resolve corporate disputes. A healthy legal system, one that ensures access, transparency and accountability, is fundamental to democracy. When the system works, the courts act as a check on government power, holding our politicians and bureaucrats to account. That is something to be applauded. In a world of spin and puff, inattention and information overload, media deregulation and TikTok, the importance of evidence and accurate information has never been so pronounced. The courts are perhaps the last remaining place where facts are primary and hyperbole is ignored. As former Queensland Supreme Court chief justice Catherine Holmes demonstrated in the Royal Commission into the Robodebt Scheme, when she reprimanded prime minister Scott Morrison, senior judges will not tolerate the dissembling that routinely occurs in other areas of public life.

Recognising the central role of the courts in determining matters that are grounded in law, but which have become too hard for the noisy political process to resolve, is what drives the work of the Grata Fund. Beyond the spin and obfuscation there are often legal principles that have been ignored. Pulling these principles back into focus is what has guided Grata's work and its decisions about which cases to support. The core aim is to help reinvigorate and buttress the court's essential democratic role in Australian society.

A decade ago, Jasmine Cavanagh, an Eastern Arrernte woman living in a remote part of the Northern Territory, asked her landlord, the territory government, to repair her toilet because it was leaking sewage through her home. The mother of a young boy, Jasmine was being forced to wake several times a night to mop up the mess, to prevent it leaking through her small home. But instead of the toilet being repaired, she was told she needed to stop throwing things into it—which she hadn't been doing. Jasmine lives in Ltyentye Apurte (Santa Teresa), about 100 kilometres down a dirt road south of Alice Springs. Like many who live in remote communities across the country, including approximately 65 000 people in the Northern Territory, she rents housing of an appalling standard. Jasmine's toilet was just one of over 600 urgent repairs requested by the community that had been ignored by the government landlord for over five years.

First Nations woman Elly Patria and her partner Dan Kelly became close to the Ltyentye Apurte community through their legal work for the Central Land Council. They became increasingly frustrated that residents, who are legal tenants of government-owned housing, were being ignored by their landlord when requesting serious and urgent repairs to their homes. As lawyers, Patria and Kelly knew that this couldn't be right, and they began a conversation with community members about their options. Seventy households decided to sue the NT Government under the *Residential Tenancies Act*, requesting urgent repairs and compensation to be paid for the loss of amenity. The government claimed that its relationship with remote community residents didn't fall under the scope of the Act and counter-sued the community for $2 million in alleged unpaid rental debts. The community persisted despite the threat.

The NT Civil and Administrative Tribunal rejected the government's claim that it didn't have responsibilities to its tenants under the *Residential Tenancies Act* and its claim for the repayment of alleged rental debts—when the government was asked for evidence of these debts, it had none. In 2018, the tribunal established that those living in the community had the right to 'habitable housing'. It defined this as 'at least safe', and ordered the government to pay its tenants damages for its repeated failure to make their houses liveable. The NT Government appealed and lost. Twice. In the process, the NT Supreme Court further clarified the standard of housing that needed to be provided. Safety was not enough. The housing had to be 'reasonably comfortable, judged against contemporary' standards.[120] The Court of Appeal further clarified that the standard was one of 'reasonableness having regard to the age, character and locality of the residential premises and to the effect of the defect on the state or condition of the premises as a whole'.[121]

As a result of its persistent failure to provide humane housing, the NT Government now has legal obligations, and owes damages, to more than 65 000 people living in substandard housing in remote communities. The High Court is currently considering whether further damages will be payable for the psychological impacts of this failure. If the court decides that residents in Ltyentye Apurte are entitled to compensation in this way, the benefits will flow to all tenants across Australia. The ramifications could also be profound for the Northern Territory's approach to remote housing and for the landlord–tenant relationship more broadly. In the meantime, the NT Government quietly wiped $69.7 million in alleged rental debts it was claiming against its residents.[122]

In many ways, this case is typical of those that Grata Fund has helped communities and their litigation teams to pursue. Assessments of potential cases are made on the basis of the underlying principle, and its application to helping create a more fulfilled, informed and active citizenry and public domain. Grata doesn't pursue class actions that are solely designed to seek financial redress—something bigger needs to be at stake. This is the reason Grata has supported doctors and the Fitzroy Legal Service to fight for their right to speak publicly about conditions on offshore detention islands, and self-described 'knitting nanas' and the Environmental Defenders Office to challenge anti-protest laws in New South Wales, and has backed a series of cases that have challenged the systemic non-disclosure of government information.

THE IMPORTANCE OF LEGAL PRINCIPLES

During the Voice referendum debate in 2023, the anti-judicial campaign found a new opportunity to engender fear of the High Court, rather than welcome its measured response to complex issues. Opponents of the Voice began to argue the proposal could have terrible implications because it could 'entangle governments in High Court cases'.[123] Janet Albrechtsen described the risk as 'opening a massive hole in parliamentary supremacy and creating a huge transfer of power from our elected parliament to unelected courts'.[124] In one of his sharper rejoinders, Greg Craven suggested that proponents of that argument would not have done well in a constitutional law exam if he'd been marking it. 'Fail. Bad fail,' he remarked.[125]

Justiciability became a word that newsreaders had to learn to get their tongues around as a small number of—mostly unnamed—constitutional lawyers, including some who otherwise supported the Voice, argued that its remit should be limited to advising the parliament, not executive government, for fear of 'clogging the courts'.

As Noel Pearson explained to the parliamentary inquiry into the Voice:

This hysteria about the role of the High Court I think is unjustified. The High Court has a role in relation to any legislation, and any citizen is allowed to go to court to test a provision, and to test the meaning of a provision.[126]

This view was shared by former High Court justices who included Robert French, Murray Gleeson and Kenneth Hayne. Solicitor-General Stephen Donaghue argued that rather than congesting the system, the Voice would enhance representative and responsible government. Nonetheless, following the Trumpian/Brexit model of ignoring inconvenient truths, the official 'No' pamphlet published by the Australian Electoral Commission in July 2023 claimed that the High Court 'would ultimately determine [the Voice body's] powers, not the Parliament. It risks legal challenges, delays and dysfunctional government'.[127]

While the campaign against the courts gathered momentum following the *Mabo* and *Wik* judgments, few would now argue that Australia is not a better place as a result of those decisions. While it may have been within the ambit of parliament to recognise native title prior to those judgments, it had failed to do so, and demonstrably would not have done so without the considered and politically impartial reasoning of the court. In this sense, the court expanded national understanding and strengthened the role of a responsible government's obligations to *all* its citizens. This is why the courts matter. They are an essential democratic institution that looks beyond the practicalities of policy to the underlying principles.

In a feverish public domain, there is little space for reasoned debate. Issues are ventilated noisily, often without context or nuance. Judges quite rightly step back from this domain, which can suggest, by omission rather than by design, that one side is 'more right'. Finding the best way to defend the courts as a democratic institution that evolves with the society it represents is crucial. This is why the intervention by former High Court judges and the solicitor-general in the legal issues associated with the capacity of the Voice to advise the executive government, as well as the parliament, was so important. As former High Court judge Michael Kirby observed years before the Voice debate:

> The feature of the Australian debate that has con-cerned many lawyers has been the complete shift from the bipartisan political acceptance of consti-tutional and other important decisions of the Court which had marked Australia's history in the past, even when those decisions were extremely important and controversial. There is also the concern that such an unrelenting barrage of criticism and denigration would, if unabated, undermine the community's confidence in the courts and acceptance of court decisions. Editorialists might declare that 'robust

legal debate [is] good for [the] country'. But a lot of judges and lawyers, unused to such unrelenting assaults, had their doubts.[128]

The Netanyahu government sparked a constitutional crisis in July 2023 by making changes to the judiciary's powers that would fundamentally alter Israeli democracy. It passed legislation to remove the ability of the judiciary to consider the reasonableness of government decisions. Proposed too (but not yet passed at the time of writing) were changes that would allow the government to 'overrule' supreme court decisions, fundamentally subverting the separation of powers. Seven months of debate in Israel preceded the move, sparking the biggest protest movement in the country's history: weekly demonstrations, highway and airport blockades, legal action, a general strike, and the threatened refusal by 10000 armed services personnel to attend duty. One would be forgiven for doubting whether the Australian public would react similarly to changes of that magnitude here. The implications of this doubt should be a reminder to those invested in Australian democracy—not only constitutional lawyers—that we must proudly engage with the role of the court in our system, and celebrate it.

~

The work of the Federal Court on country in the Torres Strait Islands earlier this year is an indication of the way the courts have kept in step with an evolving understanding of the Australian body politic. Before those fateful early hearings in *Mabo*, when the heavily gowned lawyers and judges struggled ashore each day to hear the evidence of traditional owners, this would have been unimaginable.

As Chief Justice Mortimer acknowledged in 2022 when deciding that there would be on-country hearings in relation to the lived experience of climate impacts in the Torres Strait:

> There is no denying the unremitting march of the sea onto the islands of the Torres Strait. The reality for the people of the Torres Strait is that they risk losing their way of life, their homes, their gardens, the resources of the sea on which they have always depended, and the graves of their ancestors.
>
> Whether the Commonwealth has legal responsibility for that reality, as the applicants allege in this proceeding, is a different question. However, the reality facing Torres Strait Islanders gives this proceeding some considerable urgency. The applicants, and the Torres Strait Islanders they represent, *are entitled to know whether the Commonwealth is legally responsible in the way alleged, or not.* [Emphasis added.]

This positions the court as an active and legitimate participant in decisions that go to the heart of the complexity of contemporary Australia, where pre-existing systems are deliberately acknowledged, rather than denied. Instead of threatening the stability of society, this expands understanding of the competing and complementary interests within it. The vested interests that fail to understand that this is not a zero-sum game fear they may miss out, and blame—among many others—the courts. Through this misapprehension, they place themselves at odds with the diverse interests of the Australian public, and a principle-based understanding of an evolving nation.

The calm reasoning demanded by the courts is better able to consider these competing interests than skittish politicians who may be more easily intimidated by those who may hold the purse strings of electoral success. The wheels of justice may turn slowly and expensively, but they do have the ability to cut through otherwise intractable government failures, or wilful blindness. The division of responsibility between policymaking and principle is an essential part of the system design. But timely reminders of the importance of legal principles in decision-making that impacts on democratic values we hold dear—that is something to welcome, not fear.

ACKNOWLEDGEMENTS

Thank you to Mr Conway and Ms Young, who so bravely fought for their community in Santa Teresa but did not live to see the full ramifications of their resolve.

Big *Esso* (thank you) to Uncle Pabai Pabai, Uncle Paul Kabai and their families, whose courage against all odds could change the course of history. *Mura Kalmel Sipa*—All together we stand.

Thank you, too, Aakriti Shoree and Courtney Law for your invaluable research assistance.

Finally, thank you to the small but mighty Grata Fund team, directors and donors, the communities and litigation teams we collaborate with, and my parents, husband and daughter. As Uncle Maluwap Nona always says, 'We're all part of a team. An A-team.'

NOTES

1   Chief Justice Gerard Brennan, 'Judicial Independence',
    speech, Australian Judicial Conference, 2 November
    1996, https://www.hcourt.gov.au/assets/publications/
    speeches/former-justices/brennanj/brennanj_ajc.
    htm#:~:text=Judicial%20independence%20does%20
    not%20exist,informed%20criticism%20of%20the%20
    judiciary%3F (viewed July 2023).
2   Cedric Hassing, Australian Institute of Aboriginal and
    Torres Strait Islander Studies, 'Reflections on 25 Years of
    Native Title: Interview with Justice Debra Mortimer', *Native
    Title Newsletter*, no. 2, 2017, https://aiatsis.gov.au/sites/
    default/files/research_pub/1707_nativetitlenewsletter_
    web_0_2.pdf (viewed July 2023).
3   Bryan Keon-Cohen, 'The *Mabo* Litigation: From Individual
    Claims to Communal Rights', *Monash University Law
    Review*, vol. 46, no. 3, 2020, p. 124, http://classic.austlii.
    edu.au/au/journals/MonashULawRw/2020/20.pdf (viewed
    July 2023).
4   Bryan Keon-Cohen, 'The *Mabo* Litigation: A Personal and
    Procedural Account', *Melbourne University Law Review*,
    vol. 24, no. 3, 2003, p. 935, http://classic.austlii.edu.au/au/
    journals/MelbULawRw/2000/35.html (viewed July 2023).

5   See the transcript of proceedings in Bryan Keon-Cohen (ed.), *Mabo v Queensland (No 1) and (No 2) Litigation Materials 1982–1992*, vol. 29, 1998, pp. 1038–9.

6   Keon-Cohen, 'The *Mabo* Litigation: A Personal and Procedural Account', p. 936.

7   *Mabo v Queensland [No 2]* (1992) 175 CLR 1. Herein, '*Mabo*'.

8   Dr Michael Pearson et al., 'Conservation Management Plan Volume 1: A Management Plan Consistent with s.341S(1) of the *EPBC Act 1999*', High Court of Australia, 15 March 2011, p. 201, https://www.hcourt.gov.au/assets/corporate/heritage/HCA-CMP-May2011.pdf (viewed July 2023).

9   DOCOMOMO Australia, 'NR & New International Selection Documentation Minimum Fiche', June 2014, https://docomomoaustralia.com.au/national-gallery-high-court-australia-precinct-1972-1982-act (viewed July 2023).

10   Loretta Lohberger, 'Movement Marks 50 Years of Green Politics, 40 Years since the Franklin Dam Campaign Turning Point', *ABC News*, 20 March 2022, https://www.abc.net.au/news/2022-03-20/franklin-dam-debate-divided-tasmania-but-was-key-for-the-greens/100897584 (viewed July 2023).

11   Martin Clark, interview with Michael Black AC QC, Melbourne Law School, University of Melbourne, 24 July 2013, p. 4, https://bpb-ap-se2.wpmucdn.com/blogs.unimelb.edu.au/dist/2/77/files/2013/07/Remembering-Tasmanian-Dams-Interview-Transcripts2.pdf (viewed July 2023).

12   *The Commonwealth of Australia v Tasmania* (1983) 158 CLR 1, 60 (Gibbs CJ) ('*The Tasmanian Dam Case*').

13   Tanya Josev, *The Campaign against the Courts: A History of the Judicial Activism Debate*, Federation Press, Annandale, NSW, 2017, pp. 119, 124.

14   *Farm Transparency International Ltd v State of New South Wales* (2022) 96 ALJR 655, [78] (Gageler J), summarised

by Anthony Gray, 'High Court Upholds Validity of Surveillance Devices Legislation against Freedom of Political Communication Challenge', *Australian Public Law*, 2 September 2022, https://www.auspublaw.org/blog/2022/09/high-court-upholds-validity-of-surveillance-devices-legislation-against-freedom-of-political-communication-challenge?rq=political%20communication (viewed July 2023).

15   Henry Reynolds, *Why Weren't We Told: A Personal Search for the Truth about Our History*, Viking Books, Ringwood, Vic., 1999, p. 188.

16   Jenny Hocking, 'My Mother, *Mabo*, and Me', speech, Sydney Lyceum Club, 2022.

17   *Mabo v Queensland [No 2]* (1992) 175 CLR 1, 25-31 (Brennan J), 217 (Toohey J).

18   EG Whitlam, *On Australia's Constitution*, Widescope, Camberwell, Vic., 1977, pp. 40–1.

19   Dominic Kelly, *Political Troglodytes and Economic Lunatics: The Hard Right in Australia*, La Trobe University Press, Melbourne, 2019, pp. 91, 93.

20   GE Fisher, 'External Affairs and Federalism in the Tasmanian Dam Case', *Queensland Institute of Technology Law Journal*, vol. 1, no. 1, 1985, p. 165, https://lr.law.qut.edu.au/article/download/247/240/247-1-482-1-10-20120711.pdf (viewed July 2023).

21   Kelly, *Political Troglodytes and Economic Lunatics*, pp. 91, 92.

22   *Amalgamated Society of Engineers v Adelaide Steamship Co Ltd* (1920) 28 CLR 12.

23   Kelly, *Political Troglodytes and Economic Lunatics*, p. 101.

24   Fisher, 'External Affairs and Federalism', p. 158.

25   *R v Burgess; Ex parte Henry* [1936] HCA 52, (1936) 55 CLR 608.

26   Brennan, 'Judicial Independence'.

27   *Mabo v Queensland [No 2]* (1992) 175 CLR 1, 120 (Deane & Gaudron JJ).

28 Bill Pheasant and Ian Howarth, '"Legacy of Unutterable Shame" on Land Rights', *Australian Financial Review*, 4 June 1992, https://www.afr.com/politics/legacy-of-unutterable-shame-on-land-rights-19920604-k4ydx (viewed July 2023).

29 Kelly, *Political Troglodytes and Economic Lunatics*, pp. 198, 224.

30 Josev, *The Campaign against the Courts*, pp. 134, 135.

31 Brennan, 'Judicial Independence'.

32 Josev, *The Campaign against the Courts*, p. 196.

33 Ibid., p. 155.

34 Paul Keating, 'The 10-point Plan that Undid the Good Done on Native Title', speech, Lowitja O'Donoghue Oration, University of Adelaide, 31 May 2011, http://www.paulkeating.net.au/shop/item/the-lowitja-odonoghue-oration-31-may-2011 (viewed July 2023).

35 The Howard government responded by introducing its '10 Point Plan', which was described in the Australian Human Rights Commission's 2009 *Native Title Report* as being 'now widely accepted' as having seriously undermined the 'protection and recognition of the native title rights' of Indigenous people: Aboriginal and Torres Strait Islander Social Justice Commissioner, Australian Human Rights Commission, *Native Title Report 2009*, 23 December 2009, section 1.2(a), https://humanrights.gov.au/our-work/publications/native-title-report-2009-chapter-1 (viewed July 2023).

36 Josev, *The Campaign against the Courts*, p. 155.

37 Ibid., p. 156.

38 Ibid., p. 158.

39 Justice Michael Kirby, 'Attacks on Judges: A Universal Phenomenon', speech, American Bar Association Section of Litigation Winter Leadership Meeting, Maui, Hawaii, 6 January 1998, https://www.hcourt.gov.au/assets/publications/speeches/former-justices/kirbyj/kirbyj_maui.htm (viewed July 2023).

40 Josev, *The Campaign against the Courts*, p. 173.

41 Ibid., p. 175.

42 Tony Letford, 'Yes, Refugees Are Welcome Here', *The Spectator Australia*, 20 May 2023, https://www.spectator.com.au/2023/05/yes-refugees-are-welcome-here (viewed July 2023).

43 Paul Sheehan, 'End "Lawfare" By Ditching Unworkable UN Policies', *The Sydney Morning Herald*, 8 September 2011, https://www.smh.com.au/politics/federal/end-lawfare-by-ditching-unworkable-un-policies-20110907-1jxr3.html (viewed July 2023).

44 See David Luban, 'Lawfare and Legal Ethics in Guantánamo', *Stanford Law Review*, vol. 60, 2008, pp. 1981–2026.

45 Sheehan, 'End "Lawfare"'.

46 Matthew Zagor, 'Adventures in the Grey Zone: Constitutionalism, Rights and the Review of Executive Power in the Migration Context', in John Bell and Marie-Luce Paris (eds), *Rights-Based Constitutional Review: Constitutional Courts in a Changing Landscape*, Edward Elgar, Cheltenham, UK, 2016, p. 213.

47 Gemma Jones and Alison Rehn, 'Angry Gillard Turns Fury on High Court', *The Daily Telegraph*, 2 September 2011, https://www.dailytelegraph.com.au/angry-gillard-turns-fury-on-high-court/news-story/694fcc1513d641fda7186fb26aafcbd4 (viewed July 2023).

48 Ibid.

49 *ABC News*, 'Defiant Gillard Dismisses Leadership Talk', 2 September 2011, https://www.abc.net.au/news/2011-09-02/gillard-vows-to-stay-the-course/2867622 (viewed July 2023).

50 Bianca Hall, 'Lawyers Representing Asylum Seekers Are "Un-Australian": Peter Dutton', *The Sydney Morning Herald*, 28 August 2017, https://www.smh.com.au/politics/federal/lawyers-representing-asylum-seekers-are-unaustralian-peter-dutton-20170828-gy5ci7.html (viewed July 2023).

51   See Justice Rachel Pepper and Rachael Chick, 'Ms Onus and Mr Neal: Agitators in an Age of "Green Lawfare"', *Environmental and Planning Law Journal*, vol. 35, no. 2, 2018, pp. 177–87, https://frackinginquiry.nt.gov.au/inquiry-reports?a=496018 (viewed July 2023); and Shalailah Medhora and Joshua Robertson, 'George Brandis: Vigilante Green Groups Destroying Thousands of Mining Jobs', *The Guardian*, 17 August 2015, https://www.theguardian.com/environment/2015/aug/17/george-brandis-vigilante-green-groups-destroying-thousands-of-mining-jobs (viewed July 2023).

52   Order of Justice Katzmann in *Mackay Conservation Group v The Commonwealth of Australia* (Federal Court of Australia, No. NSD33/2015, 4 August 2015), https://www.comcourts.gov.au/file/Federal/P/NSD33/2015/3715277/event/28181487/document/607760; reported in Joshua Robertson and Oliver Milman, 'Approval for Adani's Carmichael Coalmine Overturned by Federal Court', *The Guardian*, 5 August 2015, https://www.theguardian.com/australia-news/2015/aug/05/approval-for-adanis-carmichael-coalmine-overturned-by-federal-court (viewed July 2023).

53   Primrose Riordan, 'Federal Court Intervenes over Adani "Lawfare"', *Australian Financial Review*, 19 August 2015, https://www.afr.com/politics/federal-court-intervenes-over-adani-lawfare-20150819-gj2w2q (viewed July 2023).

54   Medhora and Robertson, 'George Brandis'.

55   Mark Ludlow, 'Adani's \$16b Carmichael Mine Approval Hit By "Error"', *Australian Financial Review*, 5 August 2015, https://www.afr.com/politics/adanis-16b-carmichael-mine-approval-hit-by-error-20150805-girulp (viewed July 2023).

56   Medhora and Robertson, 'George Brandis'.

57   *Federal Court of Australia Act 1976* (Cth) s 37AO.

58   Oliver Milman, 'Coalition May Change Environment Laws

after Carmichael Mine Setback', *The Guardian*, 6 August 2015, https://www.theguardian.com/environment/2015/aug/06/coalition-may-change-environment-laws-after-carmichael-mine-setback (viewed July 2023).

59   Letter from John F Eades, President of the Law Society of New South Wales, to George Brandis, Attorney-General (Cth), 18 February 2015, https://www.lawsociety.com.au/sites/default/files/2019-11/Commonwealth%20Legal%20Assistance%20Funding_Feb_2015.pdf (viewed July 2023).

60   Daniel Hurst, 'Legal Services for Vulnerable Groups Spared Cuts amid Growing Pressure', *The Guardian*, 26 March 2015, https://www.theguardian.com/australia-news/2015/mar/26/legal-services-for-vulnerable-groups-spared-cuts-amid-growing-pressure (viewed July 2023).

61   Matthew Groves, 'Lawfare and the Enemy within Our Public Law', *Australian Institute of Administrative Law Forum*, no. 90, 2017, p. 42, http://classic.austlii.edu.au/au/journals/AIAdminLawF/2017/28.html (viewed July 2023).

62   George Brandis, '"Green Lawfare" and Standing: The View from within Government', *Australian Institute of Administrative Law Forum*, no. 90, 2017, pp. 12, 14, http://classic.austlii.edu.au/au/journals/AIAdminLawF/2017/26.pdf (viewed July 2023).

63   A Odysseus Patrick, 'Australia's Aborigines Win Legal Protection against Deportation in Landmark Court Ruling', *The Washington Post*, 11 February 2020, https://www.washingtonpost.com/world/asia_pacific/australias-aborigines-win-legal-protection-against-deportation-in-landmark-court-ruling/2020/02/11/84d38d92-4c77-11ea-967b-e074d302c7d4_story.html (viewed July 2023).

64   Michael Botur, 'They Were Deported from a Country They Consider Home, to a Country They Barely Know', *Vice News*, 23 March 2022, https://www.vice.com/en/article/v7dng4/deportations-australia-new-zealand-501 (viewed July 2023).

65 Ben Doherty, '"It Starts With One Child": White-Hot Anger in New Zealand as Australia Deports 15-Year-Old', *The Guardian*, 21 March 2021, https://www.theguardian.com/australia-news/2021/mar/21/it-starts-with-one-child-white-hot-anger-in-new-zealand-as-australia-deports-15-year-old (viewed July 2023).

66 Calla Wahlquist, 'Minor Deported to New Zealand under Australian Program Peter Dutton Described As "Taking the Trash Out"', *The Guardian*, 15 March 2021, https://www.theguardian.com/australia-news/2021/mar/15/minor-deported-to-new-zealand-under-australian-program-peter-dutton-described-as-taking-the-trash-out (viewed July 2023).

67 *Love v Commonwealth of Australia; Thoms v Commonwealth of Australia*, Bell J (2020) 270 CLR 152 (at [81]), for the majority (Bell J, Gordon J, Nettle J, Edelman J).

68 Kieran Pender, 'Immigration Case Raises Concerns over High Court Politicisation', *The Saturday Paper*, 16 April 2022, https://www.thesaturdaypaper.com.au/news/politics/2022/04/09/immigration-case-raises-concerns-over-high-court-politicisation#hrd (viewed July 2023).

69 For example, *The Australian*, 'Activist High Court Takes Nation into Tricky Territory: Editorial', 13 February 2020, https://www.theaustralian.com.au/commentary/editorials/activist-high-court-takes-nation-into-tricky-territory/news-story/6c6187da7d87601ac04c71c90d40455d (viewed July 2023); and Chris Merritt, '"Lunacy Protects Foreigners over Us"', *The Australian*, 12 February 2020, https://www.theaustralian.com.au/business/legal-affairs/lunacy-protects-foreigners-over-us/news-story/274e7b2c2690ecc9023beb021ac40b26 (viewed July 2023).

70 Merritt, '"Lunacy Protects Foreigners over Us"'.

71 Chris Merritt, 'No Place for Race in the Constitution', *The Australian*, 14 February 2020, https://www.theaustralian.com.au/business/legal-affairs/no-place-for-race-in-the-constitution/news-story/3bfa8f2c19c2164c3b0f9495f864f19f (viewed July 2023).

72   James Allan, 'High Court Ruling: Activist Justices' Alien View of Court's Power', *The Australian*, 14 February 2020, https://www.theaustralian.com.au/business/legal-affairs/activist-justices-alien-view-of-courts-power/news-story/bfff4c2f860a65426dddaf5f91cf9ff6 (viewed July 2023).

73   Janet Albrechtsen, 'High Court in the Crossfire of Runaway Judicial Activism', *The Australian*, 15 February 2020, https://www.theaustralian.com.au/inquirer/high-court-in-the-crossfire-of-runaway-judicial-activism/news-story/631a06647c8216cbf7ec264e461181a9 (viewed July 2023).

74   Jennifer Oriel, 'High Court's Racist Ruling Is a Low Blow to Equality and Democracy', *The Australian*, 17 February 2020, https://www.theaustralian.com.au/commentary/high-courts-racist-ruling-is-a-low-blow-to-equality-and-democracy/news-story/2d67f520cf615f57564a14343d01577d (viewed July 2023).

75   Caroline di Russo, '*Love and Thoms*: This Isn't Closing the Gap, but Entrenching Our Differences', *The Spectator Australia*, 14 February 2020, https://www.spectator.com.au/2020/02/love-and-thoms-this-isnt-closing-the-gap-but-entrenching-our-differences (viewed July 2023).

76   Australian Bar Association, 'Australian Bar Association Calls for Respectful Discussion of the Decision in *Love*', media release, 17 February 2020, https://austbar.asn.au/news-media/australian-bar-association-calls-for-respectful-discussion-of-the-decision-in-love (viewed July 2023).

77   Marcia Langton, 'Hysteria over High Court's Ruling Is Hateful and Wrong', *The Australian*, 15 February 2020, https://www.theaustralian.com.au/inquirer/hysteria-over-high-courts-ruling-is-hateful-and-wrong/news-story/034fe0a7a578ef76b17da6e01338f3bc (viewed July 2023).

78   Chris Merritt, 'Judging the High Court's Justices', *The Australian*, 20 February 2020, https://www.theaustralian.com.au/inquirer/judging-the-high-courts-justices/news-story/6c819b096c60180d761d0ca9ab38b2eb (viewed July 2023).

79   Morgan Begg, 'Activist Judges Misrepresent *Mabo* to Create
      Privileged Class', *The Australian*, 12 February 2020, https://
      www.theaustralian.com.au/commentary/activist-judges-
      misrepresent-mabo-to-createprivileged-class/news-story/
      6c9d0372378f803a16ef6c68067bc2b1 (viewed July 2023).

80   James Allan, 'High Court of Wokeness: How on Earth
      Did the Coalition Allow This Travesty to Happen?',
      The Spectator Australia, 21 February 2020, https://www.
      spectator.com.au/2020/02/high-court-of-wokeness
      (viewed July 2023).

81   Olivia Caisley and Nicola Berkovic, '"Activism" Puts Focus
      on High Court Vacancies', *The Australian*, 20 February
      2020, https://www.theaustralian.com.au/nation/politics/
      activism-puts-focus-on-high-court-vacancies/news-story/
      9cb395e022d2950d638b5e303d0d9c0c (viewed July 2023).

82   Amanda Stoker, 'All's Fair in Love and War: The High
      Court's Decision in *Love & Thoms*', research paper,
      2021, pp. 12–16, 20, https://static1.squarespace.com/
      static/596ef6aec534a5c54429ed9e/t/5f2bab650be1946
      932e7f808/1596697467269/Senator+Amanda+Stoker+
      Paper+on+Love+June+2020.pdf (viewed July 2023).

83   George Williams, 'There Is No Place for Politics in the
      Appointment of High Court judges', *The Australian*, 15 March
      2020, https://www.theaustralian.com.au/commentary/
      there-is-no-place-for-politics-in-theappointment-of-
      high-court-judges/news-story/cb079fb6b8670df86d34ca
      7995c4c4a4 (viewed July 2023); and Judith Kelly, 'No
      Place on High Court Bench for Politics', *The Australian*,
      19 March 2020, https://www.theaustralian.com.au/business/
      legal-affairs/no-place-on-high-court-bench-for-politics/
      newsstory/61ee5b321a0e0d7f0914aee16351068f (viewed
      July 2023).

84   George Brandis, 'Diary', *The Spectator Australia*, 18 April
      2020, https://www.spectator.com.au/2020/04/diary-211
      (viewed July 2023).

85　James Paterson, 'The High Court *Love* Decision', research paper, 2020, https://static1.squarespace.com/static/596ef6aec534a5c54429ed9e/t/5f0bd1dfe9cddf559fceba69/1594610148024/Senator+James+Paterson+Paper+on+Love+July+2020.pdf (viewed July 2023).

86　*The Australian*, 'Christian Porter's High Court Challenge: Editorial', 15 October 2020, https://www.theaustralian.com.au/commentary/editorials/christian-porters-high-court-challenge/news-story/1dd258635f85de15a4ffc1efad94b63a (viewed July 2023).

87　Julian R Murphy, 'Justice Edelman's Originalism, or Hints of It', *Australian Public Law*, 6 November 2017, https://www.auspublaw.org/blog/2017/11/justice-edelmans-originalism (viewed July 2023).

88　*Commonwealth v ACT* (2013) 250 CLR 441, 455, [14].

89　Lael K Weis, 'What Comparativism Tells Us about Originalism', *International Journal of Constitutional Law*, vol. 11, no. 4, 2013, p. 842.

90　Josev, *The Campaign against the Courts*, pp. 6, 104, 105, 179.

91　Anthony Mason, 'The Centenary of the High Court in Australia', *Constitutional Law and Policy Review*, no. 5, 2003, p. 45.

92　Josev, *The Campaign against the Courts*, p. 6.

93　Ibid.

94　Ibid., p. 95.

95　Pender, 'Immigration Case Raises Concerns'.

96　Julian R Murphy and Shireen Morris, 'Changes in Policy (and Politics), Not Politicisation: The Federal Government's Decision Not to Pursue the Appeal in Montgomery', *Australian Public Law*, 16 August 2022, https://www.auspublaw.org/blog/2022/08/changes-in-policy-and-politics-not-politicisation (viewed July 2023).

97　Amanda Stoker, 'Ditched High Court Appeal against Indigenous Deportation Laws Sets a Dangerous Precedent for Foreign Criminals', *Sky News*, 1 August 2022, https://www.skynews.com.au/opinion/ditched-high-court-appeal-against-indigenous-deportation-laws-sets-a-dangerous-precedent-for-foreign-criminals/news-story/a2dfc1e8218b0b1128419a8af48bb8c0 (viewed July 2023).

98 Ronald Mizen and Michael Pelly, 'High Court Appointments a Move against "Adventurism"', *Australian Financial Review*, 28 October 2022, https://www.afr.com/politics/high-court-appointments-a-move-against-adventurism-20201021-p567a6 (viewed July 2023).

99 *LibertyWorks Inc v Commonwealth of Australia* (2021) 274 CLR 1, [249].

100 Human Rights Law Centre, 'High Court Declares Implied Freedom of Political Communication Alive and Well (Mostly)', 16 June 2021, https://www.hrlc.org.au/human-rights-case-summaries/2021/10/27/high-court-declares-implied-freedom-of-political-communication-alive-and-well-mostly (viewed July 2023).

101 *LibertyWorks Inc v Commonwealth of Australia* (2021) 274 CLR 1, [249].

102 '*Australian Capital Television v Commonwealth*: 30 Years of the Implied Freedom of Political Communication', webinar, Professor Dan Meagher, CCCS Global Public Law Seminar Series, University of Melbourne Law School, 12 September 2022, minutes 4–5, https://law.unimelb.edu.au/centres/cccs/engagement/global-public-law-seminar-series/australian-capital-television-v-commonwealth (viewed July 2023).

103 Ibid., Laureate Professor Adrienne Stone, minutes 17–18.

104 Ibid., minutes 28–29.

105 Ibid., minutes 27–28.

106 Ibid., minutes 28–29.

107 *Brown v Tasmania* (2017) 261 CLR 328, [313], [459], [465] (Gordon J).

108 *Plaintiff M47/2018 v Minister for Home Affairs* (2019) 265 CLR 285.

109 Lesley Dingle and Daniel Bates, interview with Leslie Zines, Faculty of Law, University of Cambridge, 7 October 2011, https://www.squire.law.cam.ac.uk/sites/www.law.cam.ac.uk/files/images/www.squire.law.cam.ac.uk/legacy/Media/Eminent%20Scholars%20Archive%20Transcripts/professor_leslie_zines_7_october_2011a.pdf (viewed July 2023).

110 Edwin Cameron, 'High Court of Australia Public Lecture 2017', speech, High Court of Australia, 11 October 2017, para 123, https://www.hcourt.gov.au/assets/publications/speeches/lecture-series/Cameron-Judges-Justice-and-Public-Power-Oct17.pdf (viewed July 2023).

111 Ibid., para 198.

112 Ibid., paras 215, 219.

113 Justice Michael Kirby, 'Return of the Native', speech, Australian Administrative Tribunal, 1–2 July 1996, https://www.hcourt.gov.au/assets/publications/speeches/former-justices/kirbyj/kirbyj_aat.htm#FOOTBODY_17 (viewed July 2023).

114 Jake Evans, '"Politicised" Administrative Appeals Tribunal Abolished, after Attorney-General Declares Its Reputation Ruined', *ABC News*, 16 December 2022, https://www.abc.net.au/news/2022-12-16/administrative-appeals-tribunal-abolished-by-attorney-general/101781300 (viewed July 2023).

115 Mike Seccombe, 'Odds Stacked against Justice in Politicised AAT', *The Saturday Paper*, 30 July 2022, https://www.thesaturdaypaper.com.au/news/politics/2022/07/23/odds-stacked-against-justice-politicised-aat#hrd (viewed July 2023).

116 Jennifer Strathearn, submission no. 36 to Senate Legal and Constitutional Affairs References Committee, Parliament of Australia, *Inquiry into the Performance and Integrity of Australia's Administrative Review System*, 23 November 2021, p. 1.

117 Evans, '"Politicised" Administrative Appeals Tribunal Abolished'.

118 Julian Leeser, 'Introduction', *Upholding the Australian Constitution: The Samuel Griffith Society Proceedings*, 23rd Conference of the Samuel Griffith Society, 2011, p iii, http://classic.austlii.edu.au/au/journals/SGSocUphAUCon/2011/1.html (viewed July 2023).

119 Aaron Patrick and Michael Pelly, '"He's the Smartest Lawyer I've Ever Met"', *Australian Financial Review*, 28 October 2020, https://www.afr.com/work-and-careers/leaders/he-s-the-smartest-lawyer-i-ve-ever-met-20201028-p569dn (viewed July 2023).

120 *Young & Conway v Chief Executive Officer, Housing* (2020) 355 FLR 290, [80].

121 *Chief Executive Officer (Housing) v Young & Anor* [2022] NTCA 1, [50].

122 Michael Park and Dijana Damjanovic, '$70 Million in Remote Rent Debts "Quietly" Written Off in the Northern Territory', *NITV News*, 12 October 2022, https://www.sbs.com.au/nitv/nitv-news/article/70-million-in-remote-rent-debts-quietly-written-off-in-the-northern-territory/kylykxm9u (viewed July 2023).

123 Chris Mitchell, 'Raging Moral Coercion on the Indigenous Voice to Parliament is Failing', *The Australian*, 16 April 2023, https://www.theaustralian.com.au/business/media/raging-moral-coercion-on-voice-is-failing/news-story/e3dc9a7cce2ce0fd85bd525ba30d0e7d (viewed July 2023).

124 Janet Albrechtsen, 'Court in the Act: What Else Is Voice Lobby Not Telling Us?', *The Australian*, 1 March 2023, https://www.theaustralian.com.au/commentary/court-in-the-act-what-else-is-voice-lobby-not-telling-us/news-story/f279b11b87c561cd199291232b513aa4 (viewed July 2023).

125 Greg Craven, 'Chicken Littles Are Wrong: Voice Won't Make Legal Sky Fall', *The Australian*, 18 August 2022,

https://www.theaustralian.com.au/commentary/chicken-littles-are-wrong-voice-wont-make-legal-sky-fall/news-story/b8a5dcd9e8f1367001f0b4b471d0d943 (viewed July 2023).

126 Evidence to Joint Select Committee on the Aboriginal and Torres Strait Islander Voice Referendum (Noel Pearson, Director, Cape York Institute), Parliament of Australia, Canberra, 1 May 2023, p. 41, https://parlinfo.aph.gov.au/parlInfo/download/committees/commjnt/26826/toc_pdf/Aboriginal%20and%20Torres%20Strait%20Islander%20Voice%20Referendum%20Joint%20Select%20Committee_2023_05_01_Official.pdf;fileType=application%2Fpdf#search=%22committees/commjnt/26826/0000%22 (viewed July 2023).

127 Australian Government, *Your Official Yes/No Referendum Pamphlet*, 2023, https://www.aec.gov.au/referendums/files/pamphlet/your-official-yes-no-referendum-pamphlet.pdf?=v1.0 (viewed July 2023).

128 Kirby, 'Attacks on Judges'.

IN THE NATIONAL INTEREST

Other books on the issues that matter: